In Touch with the Word

Lectionary-Based
Prayer Reflections

In Touch with the Word

Lectionary-Based Prayer Reflections

Cycle A for Ordinary Time

Lisa-Marie Calderone-Stewart

Saint Mary's Press
Christian Brothers Publications
Winona, Minnesota

- Thank you, Fr. Bob Stamschror, for your constant affirmation and guidance in this project, and in all the projects we envision and accomplish together. It is a joy to work with you.
- Thank you, Ralph, for the love and care you give me every day, as well as the technical assistance I need whenever our computer doesn't understand what I want it to do.
- Thank you, Bishop Ken Untener. You have had a major influence on my spiritual formation, my ministry, and my life.

 Genuine recycled paper with 10% post-consumer waste. Printed with soy-based ink.

The publishing team for this book included Robert P. Stamschror, development editor; Laurie A. Berg, copy editor; Lynn Dahdal, production editor; Hollace Storkel, typesetter; Stephan Nagel and Kent Linder, cover designers; Maurine R. Twait, art director; pre-press, printing, and binding by the graphics division of Saint Mary's Press.

The acknowledgments continue on page 132.

Printed in the United States of America

Printing: 9 8 7 6 5 4 3 2 1

Year: 2006 05 04 03 02 01 00 99 98

ISBN 0-88489-545-9, paper
ISBN 0-88489-576-9, spiral

To my mother:
Thank you, thank you, thank you
for life, for love, for joy.
It is so much fun being your daughter!
You give me great ideas,
wise insights,
constructive feedback,
unconditional support,
and weekly laughter.
The best part about being an author
is your pride and enthusiasm with each new book!
I love you, Mom!

Contents

Introduction

Did you ever go to Mass on Sunday, listen to the Scripture readings, and then promptly forget what they were all about or how your life relates to their message? Does this sound familiar? Even though you may have listened to a homilist who connected the word with you and challenged you at that time, what about the week before the Sunday Scriptures or the week after? How can you anticipate and prepare for the word? How can you stay in touch with the word that was heard?

This book is a resource designed to do just that—to help you prepare for the Sunday Scripture readings and to help you stay in touch with the word.

Using This Book

Using *In Touch with the Word* is a simple procedure. First, decide which Sunday's readings you are going to share. If it is Friday afternoon, you might want to reflect on the readings for the next Sunday so you can be more prepared for the upcoming liturgy. If it is Monday morning, you might want to remember the readings you heard on Sunday so you can stay in touch with that word the rest of the week. Next, turn to the page for the Sunday you have in mind. There you will find reflections, questions, and a prayer based on that Sunday's readings.

The Sunday Scripture Readings

The Scripture readings for each Sunday are found in a book called a lectionary. The Sunday readings follow a three-year, A-B-C cycle that continues to repeat itself. The readings in the A cycle highlight the Gospel of Matthew. The readings in the B cycle highlight the Gospel of Mark. The readings in the C cycle highlight the Gospel of Luke. (If you are wondering about the Gospel of John, don't be concerned. His readings are woven throughout all three years on special days that seem to need that "John" touch.)

The church calendar year consists of the seasons of Advent and Christmas, Lent and Easter, plus Ordinary Time. This book covers Ordinary Time, A cycle only. (The Sundays of B and C cycle in Ordinary Time, and the Sundays of the Advent, Christmas, Lent, and Easter seasons will be found in other volumes of this series.) Most Sundays have three sets of readings, one for each cycle. But in this book you will find only the readings for the A cycle. The dates for each Sunday in the A cycle are given for the next several years.

You will note that the Scripture readings are not reprinted in this book. It would make the book too big and too expensive. You will need either a lectionary or a Bible to read one or more of the Scripture readings as part of the prayer reflection. However, a capsulated version of each Scripture reading is provided.

One of the three Scripture readings listed with each Sunday has an open bullet (○) next to it. This indicates which reading will be most focused on in the reflection and which one you might want to read as part of the reflection.

Theme

A summary of a central theme of the readings is also offered. You may want to use it to set a context for the reflection questions that will initiate sharing of and reflection on the word.

Reflections

The reflection questions for each Sunday address audiences in three categories: adults, teenagers, and children. However, feel free to cross categories in the use of the questions whenever it is appropriate.

Focusing Object

For each set of readings, you will find a suggested focusing object. Using a focusing object in these prayer reflections is not mandatory, but it is helpful, especially with teenagers and children. It is a visual, hands-on reminder of the readings and their message. For example, anticipating or recalling the meaning of the passage about our relationship with Jesus being like a vine and its branches is much easier and more vivid if a plant with a stem and branches is present when reflecting on the reading of that passage.

The focusing object is handy for facilitating the prayer reflection and sharing. For example, after the Scripture reading is proclaimed, the facilitator asks one of the reflection questions for everyone to think about and share their thoughts. Then the facilitator picks up the focusing object and begins the sharing. When finished, the facilitator passes the object to the next person who is ready to share.

The focusing object can be passed around a circle, so everyone knows when their turn is coming, or it can be passed randomly as people become ready to share. A large group does better sitting in a circle and passing the object around in order. In a small group—one that fits around a table where everyone can reach the middle—anyone who is ready can pick up the object, share, and replace it for the next person who is ready to take a turn. Also, using the object makes it obvious when a person's turn has ended—no one has to guess. If someone just wants to offer a one-word response, or even remain silent, the focusing object is simply handed to the next person.

The focusing object is more than a reminder or a turn-designator. It is also an effective way to reduce the self-conscious feeling many people get when they are expected to share with a group of their peers. Persons handling an object and looking at it tend to relax and forget that a roomful of people are watching them. People who are relaxed and comfortable do a better job of sharing. This is true of adults, teenagers, and children!

After everyone has had a chance to share, the object comes back to the facilitator, who ends with the "Closing" or any other words she or he feels would be appropriate.

The focusing object can stay on a kitchen table or a classroom shelf all week, acting as a reminder of God's word and the people's response.

Closing

A closing is provided for each prayer reflection. It consists of a poem or reading that ends the reflections with an inspirational touch. You will notice that the closings come from a variety of cultures, and each culture adds a rich spiritual tradition to the prayer reflections.

Indexes

Each Sunday's prayer session is indexed by focusing object and by theme in the back of this book.

Settings

Parish

Parish staffs, councils, and committees usually want to start their meetings with some type of prayer. Prayer based on Sunday's readings is a great way to help the group relate to the parish liturgy, connect with the message of the Sunday readings, and start the meeting off on a spiritual plane.

Homilists can benefit from this resource by looking at the message through the eyes of adults, teenagers, and children. This can provide a springboard for the type of insights needed to be pastoral, effective, and challenging to the assembly of mixed ages that typically gathers each Sunday. (Actually sharing the reflection questions with adults, teenagers, and children and listening to their responses each week provides even better feedback for a homilist!)

Liturgy planning groups will find this book helpful. Members with different degrees of liturgical experience and understanding can read the theme summaries, share the questions, and get a feel for the flow of the Scriptures. The suggested focusing object can also remind the group to investigate the possibilities of symbolism in the physical environment of the worship space.

Prayer groups and small Christian communities will find *In Touch with the Word* very helpful, especially if the groups include families with children of different ages.

Youth Groupings

Youth ministers will find the prayer reflections in this book a simple way to prepare a youth group or team for the readings they will hear the following Sunday or feast day and to help them stay in touch with the readings they heard the previous Sunday. At the same time, the reflections call attention to the major seasons of the church year. The prayer process in the reflection works equally well with junior high teens or high school teens.

Parish religious education teachers and catechists meeting with a class once a week can use this resource to relate to the Sunday and feast day readings. Sending a note home each week encouraging parents to discuss the readings with their children at the dinner table or at bedtime, perhaps with a similar focusing object, is a good way to weave a family connection into a parish religious education program.

Religion teachers in Catholic schools looking for a way to connect students with their parish community will value this resource. Anticipating or recalling the Scriptures read at the parish liturgies will help students stay in touch with their parish community.

Families

Busy families will find that using *In Touch with the Word* at home is a great way to make liturgical worship more relevant for their teenagers or younger children. Using the prayer reflections does not take long and is easy to do. Best of all, it helps the family as a whole connect with what is said at Mass and remember it throughout the week. Parents may find their teenagers more likely to share prayer if they are doing it "for the sake of their younger brothers and sisters" than if they think they are doing it for themselves!

Parishes with family-based programming can use this resource in several ways. If the parish supplies families with resources to be used at home, every family can receive a copy of *In Touch with the Word* to use on their own. If families gather regularly at the parish for a scheduled activity, the sharing process can be incorporated with the program. If family groups meet in cells or units, they can be provided with copies of this book and suggestions for how it can be used in the context of their meeting.

Whether you work with adults, teenagers, or children in a parish, school, or home setting, you will find that being in touch with the word is easy with *In Touch with the Word.*

Trinity Sunday

30 May 1999
26 May 2002
22 May 2005

Communication

Scripture

- *Exodus 34:4–6,8–9.* Moses approaches God humbly, yet boldly requests that God pardon the sins of the stiff-necked Israelites. God speaks the Divine Name three times.
- *2 Corinthians 13:11–13.* Paul's letter ends with a trinitarian formula.
- *John 3:16–18.* God, who is the source and parent, sends Jesus, the Redeemer and only Son, to save the world, so that through the power of the Holy Spirit, believers may know God and have eternal life.

Theme

The Trinity is a mystery, impossible to fully understand. So we often speak in analogy or try to use words that reflect a unified threesome. God our Maker is indeed a God of compassion and forgiveness. In the Gospel, John pulls together the relationship of God, our compassionate and forgiving maker, with Jesus the Son, who is also God and our Redeemer. And Paul, in the second reading, refers to God as Maker, Jesus, and the Holy Spirit together in his greeting in the name of God as Trinity.

Focusing Object

A greeting card

Reflections

Paul sends greetings, and he encourages us to greet one another with a holy kiss. Paul ends with a trinitarian blessing for grace, love, and fellowship. Greetings, blessings, and prayers are almost inseparable in a Christian community. People greet one another, support one another, and bid farewell, all in the name of God. Communication with God and communication with brothers and sisters in Christ appear to be the same thing. With such a community philosophy, prayer is second nature. God is always the focus. Everything is said and done with the spirit of faith and love.

• How is the community of that description similar to or different from the everyday community you experience?

Prayer is communication with God. God is always communicating with us—we are surrounded by God's love and care. Yet we don't always seem to be aware of God's presence and connection with us. Usually it is up to us to open the channels so that God's communication can flow to us.

• How easy or difficult is it for you to open up those channels?

• How would you describe your prayer life? As rich and fulfilling? dry and barren? fragile but growing?

The second reading is like a greeting card from Paul. It is a note of encouragement and love. In Paul's day they don't have "smiley faces" that say, "Have a nice day," but Paul still cares enough to send the very best. He sends greetings and blessings in the name of God as Trinity—our Creator, our Savior Jesus, and the Spirit they share. We share in that holy and divine Spirit whenever we greet and bless one another.

• When was the last time you sent someone a greeting card that your parents didn't make you send?

- When was the last time you received a card that wasn't a Christmas or birthday card?

Prayer is like a greeting card to God and from God. Greeting cards do not create love and friendship between people, but they are a channel so that feelings and thoughts can be shared and expressed more easily.

- What feelings and thoughts does God express to you? How do you know?
- What feelings and thoughts do you express to God? How do you do it?

For Children

Lots of people like to send and receive greeting cards.

- Do you like getting Christmas cards and birthday cards?
- Who sends you Christmas cards and birthday cards?
- Do you ever get any other cards? If so, when? from whom?
- Do you ever send cards? If so, to whom?
- What kinds of things do you like to write in the cards you send?

Praying is like sending God a greeting card. Praying is also like receiving a greeting card from God.

- If you could actually mail a card to God, what would you write on it?
- What do you think God would write on a card to you?

Closing

Prayer is like the turning on
of an electric switch.
It does not create the current;
it simply provides a channel
through which the current can flow.
                              —Max Handel
                         (Vision 2000: A Cycle)

Feast of the Body and Blood of Christ

6 June 1999
2 June 2002
29 May 2005

Food for Life

Scripture

- *Deuteronomy 8:2–3,14–16.* God sends manna and water to the starving and thirsting Israelites in the desert so that they will not die.
- *1 Corinthians 10:16–17.* The bread we eat and the wine we drink are a sharing in the flesh and blood of Jesus, the Christ. We eat of one loaf, and we are one Body of Christ.
- *John 6:51–58.* Jesus, the Christ, is the bread of life. If we eat his flesh and drink his blood, we will live forever.

Theme

The Israelites in the desert are given the fine white flakes of manna on the ground to eat and water from a rock to drink so that they will not die. In a similar way, Jesus gives us his own flesh to eat and his blood to drink so that we will not die. Our unity as one is symbolized by the one loaf.

Focusing Object
Bread and wine

Reflections

It is a mystery how simple bread and wine becomes the actual flesh and blood of Jesus, the Christ. We cannot understand it because it is beyond our comprehension. But we call that miracle feast *Eucharist,* which actually means "giving thanks."

- Are you usually aware of the food and drink you are consuming at every meal, or do you take eating and drinking for granted?
- Do you usually say a blessing before each meal? Why or why not? Does the setting make a difference? For instance, does it matter if you are at a family meal with children present, or if you are at a restaurant with business colleagues? Why or why not?

Our eating of the flesh and blood of Jesus, the Christ, and our being the Body of Christ have great symbolism. When we celebrate the Eucharist, we eat from one loaf and drink from one cup. The loaf is made up of many different ingredients that combine to form a completely different union. We are different people who come together at the Eucharist to form a spiritual union. The one loaf does not nourish anyone unless it is broken apart and given to different people to partake of it. As the Body of Christ, we take our differences and even our brokenness and go forth to do good works for other people. When we eat bread and drink wine, that food becomes part of our body chemistry. When we eat the bread and drink the wine that are the body and blood of Jesus, the Christ, Jesus becomes part of our spiritual chemistry.

- How are you changed by the parish Eucharist?
- How is your parish changed by your participation in the Eucharist?
- How are those two questions related?

For Teenagers

Jesus tells us that he is the living bread of life, and that those of us who eat his flesh and drink his blood will live forever. We call that meal the Eucharist; this name means "giving thanks."

- Are you thankful for the abundance of food in your life? Or do you take it for granted?
- How often have you gotten ready for an evening meal (after eating once or twice already that day) and said, "I'm starving!"
- How often do you think of people who only have one tiny meal to eat all day? When you do think of them, how do your thoughts affect you?

The symbol of the meal is significant. In Jesus' time every item of food had to be prepared, and the ingredients needed to be gathered and used before they spoiled. Preparing and cooking food for a meal was a major job.

- What do you think is the overall attitude of teenagers regarding food, nutrition, and health? Are most teens careful not to eat junk food—or is junk food their main form of nutrition?
- Is there a problem in your area with obesity? How about anorexia? bulimia?
- How are today's meals and meal preparation procedures different from the meals and their preparation in Jesus' time?

For Children

At special meals people often eat special bread and drink special wine. Mass is a special meal, and the bread and wine at Mass are very special. They are special because they are no longer ordinary bread and wine. They have become the body and blood of Jesus, the Christ.

- Do you receive Communion yet? If so, what is it like? What was your first Communion like?
- If you don't receive Communion yet, do you know how old you will be when you do? Do you think that will be an exciting and important day? Why or why not?
- *Eucharist* means "giving thanks." Why do we need to say a blessing prayer before we eat a meal and a prayer of thanks after we eat? Whom are we thanking?

- Does everyone in the world have enough food to eat, or are some children and grown-ups always hungry? Why is it a good idea to pray for hungry people?

Closing

Whoever eats food without giving thanks steals from God. —An old Jewish saying

(Action 2000: C Cycle)

Second Sunday of the Year

17 January 1999
20 January 2002
16 January 2005

Light for All Nations

Scripture

- ○ *Isaiah 49:3,5–6.* Isaiah tells us that God formed Israel to be a light to all peoples, so that salvation might be spread to all nations.
- • *1 Corinthians 1:1–3.* Paul greets and encourages the Corinthians.
- • *John 1:29–34.* John the Baptizer tells how he did not recognize Jesus until he saw the Spirit descend like a dove and rest on Jesus.

Theme

The "suffering servant" song from Isaiah echoes the same message as the Gospel story—that Jesus is the Chosen One, who is to bring light and salvation to all nations and all peoples. Paul's letter reminds us that as a holy people, as followers of Jesus, we share in that mission.

Focusing Object
A flashlight

Reflections

For Adults

Paul, Isaiah, and John the Baptizer all responded to God's call. As Jesus' followers, we are also called to continue his mission and to be light for all nations.
- • What does it mean to be light for all nations?

- How can ordinary people continue the mission of Jesus?
- Who are people you know that are light for others? Who are people that shine in their commitment to faith? Who are the ordinary people that are like modern saints in your world?

Isaiah speaks of the Lord as one who forms servants in the womb. The womb is a place of complete darkness, complete isolation, and complete mystery. Yet we are called from that place of darkness to be light. So often, we who have spent time in darkness can best be light for others. We who have been broken can bring healing to others. We who have known hunger can feed others.

- When have you, having been in a particular situation, been able to serve others in similar situations?
- When have you, in a particular situation, been served by others who have had similar experiences?

For Teenagers

John the Baptizer doesn't just sit on a rock when he receives the call from God. Paul doesn't just sit. Isaiah doesn't just sit around, either. They are called to do God's work, and so they get up and start working. Isaiah proclaims truth and warnings; Paul travels, establishes churches, and writes letters; John baptizes and preaches repentance.

- How does a teenager do God's work?
- Why aren't more teenagers (or adults) involved in God's work?

As followers of Jesus, we are called to be light to all nations. In Isaiah's time that had a specific and serious meaning. It meant that salvation would be brought to all peoples, not just to the Jews. This was a hard message for many Jews to accept. Jews believed that they were God's Chosen People and that they needed to avoid other, "lesser" peoples in order to remain true to God's way.

- Today many Americans act as if they believe they are God's new chosen people. It is difficult for them to accept foreign peoples and foreign ways. What evidence do you see of that in the news?
- Do you have "chosen people" in your school? Are some groups shunned as "lesser"? If so, why? Where do those attitudes come from? How are you called to be a light to all peoples—even to students in your high school who are in shunned groups?

For Children

God wants us to be light to all people. When a light shines, it makes everything easier to see and to do. It's very hard to do anything in the dark.
- How can you be like a light and make things easier for your family?
- How can you be like a light and make things easier for everyone in your class?
- How can you be like a light and make things easier for people in your neighborhood?

Closing

Nothing can dim the light which shines from within. —Maya Angelou

(Acts of Faith)

Third Sunday of the Year

24 January 1999
27 January 2002
23 January 2005

Call to Discipleship

Scripture

- *Isaiah 8:23—9:3.* Isaiah brings great news to people. Those who were in darkness are now walking in the light. Those who were in gloom are now rejoicing with joy.
- *1 Corinthians 1:10–13,17.* Paul begs Christians to be united and not divided.
- *Matthew 4:12–23.* Jesus calls his first disciples right from their fishing boats. They immediately follow him.

Theme

We have opportunities we must respond to without delay. Simon, Andrew, James, and John immediately abandon their nets to follow Jesus without delay. We do not have time to waste in the darkness and gloom. It is time to unite and to recognize Jesus as the One who unites us. It is time to walk in the light, dance with joy, and be fishers of men and women for Jesus.

Focusing Object
A fish

Reflections

For Adults

The four fishermen of this Gospel story do not hesitate when Jesus calls them to follow him but immediately drop their nets and leave behind fish, boat, and even father. That is how inviting Jesus is. Suddenly they see the light, and their priorities change instantly.

- Has there been a time in your life when something happened to change all your priorities, when things that had seemed important were suddenly not important at all?
- What do you suppose made four fishermen leave their life's work because a stranger invited them?

Following Jesus sounds easy, but many followers of Jesus disagree on matters of faith.

- Is all this disagreement healthy or unhealthy for the church? Why?
- Do disagreements and dialog confuse us about the truth, or do they lead us to the truth?

For Teenagers

Simon, Andrew, James, and John drop their nets the second that Jesus shows up. They leave their fish and boats in the water and start a whole new life. Imagine Zebedee's thoughts as he watches his two sons walk off with someone he knows little about.

- What would your parents say if you tried to do something like that?
- How could you explain the importance of following Jesus to your parents if they had never heard of him or knew little about him?

These four fishermen did not miss the chance to answer Jesus' invitation.

- "Strike while the iron is hot" and "Opportunity knocks but once" are old sayings. Have you heard these sayings before? What do they really mean?
- Have you ever chosen to take advantage of an opportunity right away, and it turned out to be a good decision? If so, when? What happened?

- Have you ever chosen to take advantage of what you thought was a good opportunity, and it turned out to be a bad decision? If so, when? What happened?
- How can you begin to tell the good opportunities from the bad ones?

For Children

Jesus was walking along the Sea of Galilee, and he saw four fishermen. He asked the first two—Simon and his brother Andrew—to follow him, and they did so right away. Then he called the second two— James and John—to do likewise, and they did so right away, too.

- The four men did not know much about Jesus at this point. What do you suppose they were thinking when they left their fishnets and their boats to follow Jesus?
- Jesus told them that they would be fishing for men and women instead of for fish. What do you think that means?
- Have you ever gone fishing? If so, what is it like? If not, would you like to try it? Why or why not?

Closing

If there is any kindness I can show, or any good thing I can do to any fellow being, let me do it now, and not deter or neglect it, as I shall not pass this way again. —William Penn

(Random Acts of Kindness)

Fourth Sunday
of the Year

31 January 1999
3 February 2002
30 January 2005

✝umility

Scripture

- *Zephaniah 2:3; 3:12–13.* The prophet urges us to be humble and to seek justice.
- *1 Corinthians 1:26–31.* Paul reminds us that God chooses the weak and those considered absurd, to shame the strong and the wise.
- *Matthew 5:1–12.* Jesus teaches us that those who are happy and most blessed are those who are humble, lowly, merciful, sorrowing, and persecuted.

Theme

The message of humility is clearly expressed in all three of these readings. The humble ones are the ones who do not sin and who do not tell lies. The humble ones are those who shame the proud ones by their humility. The humble ones are the ones who are happiest and most blessed.

Focusing Object
A happy face

Reflections

For Adults

In Tanzania, the Luo tribe calls God Nyasay Niakalaga, which means Creator, Originator, Source. God created us and is the origin and source of all that we are. Consequently, people often ask, Why would God create us so imperfect?

- What is the connection between imperfect beings and humility?
- What is the connection between imperfect beings and sinfulness in the world?
- What is the connection between sinfulness and pride?
- What is the connection between pride and humility?
- How is it that we can be most blessed and most happy if we are poor in spirit, sorrowing, lowly, and so on? How can today's Gospel verses, which are called the Beatitudes, make any sense?
- How is the message of our modern American culture different from the message of the Beatitudes?

For Teenagers

The verses of today's Gospel are called the Beatitudes. Sometimes they are called the Be Attitudes because they tell us the kind of attitudes we need to develop and the way we need to be.

- Do these Beatitudes sound like good news or bad news? Why?
- Who are the most peaceful and contented people you know? What do they have in common with the attitudes of the Beatitudes?
- What are the attitudes of consumerism and materialism? How do commercials and ads encourage people to buy products? How are these attitudes different from those of the Beatitudes?
- What attitudes would make a better world? What attitudes would make a more selfish and self-centered world?
- How could you rewrite the Beatitudes in language that most teenagers today would more easily understand?

For Children

Jesus tells us that the times we feel sad can be the times we can do good—for example, when we feel sorrowful, when we see fighting, or when we see others being made fun of.

• What are some situations that make you feel sad about what is happening? What can you do to make things better?

Closing

Most folks are about as happy as they make up their minds to be. —Abraham Lincoln

(A greeting card message)

Fifth Sunday of the Year

7 February 1999
10 February 2002
6 February 2005

Light and Salt for the World

Scripture

- *Isaiah 58:7–10.* If we share our food and home and clothing with the poor, then our light will break forth like the dawn and God will help us.
- *1 Corinthians 2:1–5.* The power of God cannot be understood with the wisdom of human beings.
- *Matthew 5:13–16.* We are salt and light for the world.

Theme

Five of the last six Sundays since Epiphany have had readings from Isaiah, and all of those five have used light as a symbol and image. Two of the Gospels have used it as well. In today's Gospel we are told directly that we are light for the world and salt for the earth. The power of light comes from God, and though we can see its effect, our limited human mind cannot comprehend it.

Focusing Object

A burning candle and a container of salt

Reflections

For Adults

We are familiar with this Gospel; it is a favorite. The symbols of light and salt speak to us today, for even in a modern world, we still need light and salt to operate. We need light to see and salt to flavor our food.

- Light aids our vision and allows us to work more efficiently. When have you helped someone see things more clearly? When has your help made a group's work more efficient?
- Salt seasons and preserves food; it is a catalyst for burning fuel. When have you preserved life? When have you added spice to life? When have you been a catalyst for action that needed a boost in order to start happening?
- Who are the people in your life who are salt and light? How have you learned from them?

Jesus talks of salt that has lost its flavor and lights that are hidden under baskets.

- When have you burned out and "lost your flavor"? What did you do? What can anyone do in that situation?
- When someone you know is suffering from burnout, what can you do to help? What are the symptoms? How can you help someone notice the symptoms?
- When have you hidden your talents?
- When have you seen others hide their talents?
- How have you helped others discover their talents and use them?

Too much of a good thing can be a bad thing. Too much salt in your diet is unhealthy. Too much light is blinding.

- How do you find balance in a world of extremes?

For Teenagers

Salt is a preservative and a flavor agent for food. Salt used to be rare and difficult to mine, but it is found in almost every kitchen today.

- Why does Jesus compare us to salt?
- Who is an adult that is like salt to the world— someone who makes life more flavorful? How have you learned from this adult?

Because salt is a key ingredient in the many instant, canned, and prepared foods they consume, most Americans eat too much salt, and many are at risk for high blood pressure.

- Do you know what your blood pressure is? When did you last have it checked?
- What are your favorite foods? Are you aware of how much sodium (salt) they contain?
- Do you put salt on food before you even taste it?
- When it comes to salt, it is possible to have too much of a good thing. If we are like salt, what might be the "good things" we have too much of?

Light is essential in order for us to see. When the sun goes down, we generally rely on electricity to light up our life.

- What is the longest your home has ever gone without electricity? How did you cope?
- Besides electric lights, what things would you have to do without if your home lost electric power for a week?
- Why does Jesus compare us to light?
- Who has been light for you—who has helped bring you out of the darkness? How have you learned from this person? How did that learning take place?

For Children

Jesus says that we are like salt and light for the world. Salt gives us flavor, and light helps us to see.

- What foods do you like to sprinkle salt on? What foods are already salty enough?
- When do you put lights on in your house? What do the lights look like? Do they hang from the ceiling, or do they sit on tables?

Being salt for the world is like bringing flavor to the world. Being light for the world is like doing good things that shine for the world. Being like light and salt is like being a teacher for others to see and to learn from.

- Who are your favorite teachers?
- What have you learned from them?
- Have you ever taught anything to anyone?

Closing

Education is hanging around until you've caught on. —Robert Frost

(Familiar Quotations)

Sixth Sunday of the Year

14 February 1999

The readings for this Sunday do not occur in 2002 or 2005.

Dealing with Feelings

Scripture

- *Sirach 15:15–20.* We have the power of choice; it is up to us to choose wisely.
- *1 Corinthians 2:6–10.* The wisdom of God is mysterious; faith in the Spirit will lead us to God's ways, because our own human wisdom is not enough for us to understand them.
- *Matthew 5:17–37.* We are warned against not only evil deeds but also evil thoughts, which may lead to evil deeds. Even if you do not intend to kill or hurt a person, you must still dissolve your anger against him or her, and you must not lay your gift at the altar until the two of you are reconciled.

Theme

God's ways are mysterious. God's decision to give us free choice seems mysterious, because we can choose evil as well as good. Jesus warns us not only to avoid murder but also to avoid anger, not only to avoid adultery but also to avoid lustful thoughts, not only to avoid false swearing but also to avoid all swearing. Good thoughts will lead to good actions and good habits.

Focusing Object

An upside-down happy face

Reflections

For Adults

Of all the warnings in this Gospel reading, the one that is usually the most difficult to deal with is getting rid of the feelings that can prompt bad action. For example, don't even bother with the gift at the altar while you are still angry; leave it, and return to reconcile. This is particularly difficult for families who have to scramble to get ready for Mass. Disagreements occur over who can use the bathroom when, who can wear which clothes, who needs to clean up which mess, and sometimes even who will attend which Mass.

• Do you have any memories of family chaos surrounding going to Mass? Are they recent or distant memories? How did they affect your readiness for the Eucharist?

Contradiction exists in the world about the role of anger. Some say that anger is dangerous, and that it needs to be controlled and avoided and not expressed. Others say that anger is a feeling, and that feelings are neither good nor bad as long as they are expressed appropriately.

• How do you see anger? Is it dangerous? Is it normal and healthy?
• How do you deal with your own anger?

For Teenagers

This Gospel reading urges us not to use abusive language and not to remain angry with our brothers and sisters.

• Do you have any brothers or sisters? If so, how do you get along? Do you ever exchange angry words? How do you reconcile?
• How about your parents or guardians—how do you get along with them? What happens after angry words?
• How about your friends—do you ever exchange angry words with them? How do you reconcile?

- Are your tolerance level and your apology style with your friends different from those with your brothers and sisters or with your parents or guardians? If so, how do they differ?

A lot of rage and violence are expressed in songs on the radio and in movies and TV shows. Many teenagers prefer to claim that watching violent shows or listening to violent songs has no connection to the violence in our world, but many others know better.

- What parallel do you see between the amount of violence and rage in the media and the amount of violence in the real world? What is the connection?
- What do you know of "copycat crimes" that have occurred because someone is imitating an act seen on television, in the movies, or in the news?
- How is Jesus' warning to avoid not only murder but even anger related to the level of violence in today's world?

For Children

Jesus tells us to be careful of what we do and to also be careful of what we think and say. Sometimes we think a bad thought, then we say a bad thing, and then we end up doing a bad thing.

- We can also think good thoughts, and then say and do good things. When have you done that?

Jesus asks us to apologize to people we have been fighting with, especially when we are on our way to church.

- Why is it hard to pray when we are angry with someone?
- Is there anyone that you fight with a lot? If so, what do you usually fight about? What can you do about it?

Closing

You cannot shake hands with a clenched fist.
—Indira Gandhi

(The Promise of a New Day)

Seventh Sunday of the Year

The readings for this Sunday do not occur in 1999, 2002, or 2005.

Love Your Enemies

Scripture

- *Leviticus 19:1–2,17–18.* Imitate God's holiness and do not sin. Love others.
- *1 Corinthians 3:16–23.* You are the temple of the Holy Spirit. Be holy.
- ○ *Matthew 5:38–48.* Offer no resistance to injury. Love your enemies.

Theme

Holiness and love are proclaimed with today's readings. But Jesus takes us a step further. We are to strive to be perfect. The old law to take "an eye for an eye and a tooth for a tooth" is no longer our law. We are to love even our enemies. We are to give to those who take from us and to let people hit us a second time after they have hit us a first time.

Focusing Object
A toothbrush

Reflections

For Adults

Some people try to use the Bible verse about taking "an eye for an eye and a tooth for a tooth" to justify capital punishment, but that is simply a case of inappropriate interpretation. Jesus, an innocent victim of the death penalty, clearly spoke against violence of any kind.

People against the death penalty can officially make their wishes known by signing the Declaration of Life, a two-page statement requiring notarization that says, "I hereby declare that should I die as a result of a violent crime, I request that the person or persons found guilty of homicide for my killing not be subject to or put in jeopardy of the death penalty under any circumstances, no matter how heinous their crime or how much I may have suffered." (To obtain a copy of the Declaration of Life, send a stamped, self-addressed envelope to Cherish Life Circle, Convent of Mercy, 273 Willoughby Avenue, Brooklyn, NY 11205.)

For Teenagers

The old law about taking "an eye for an eye and a tooth for a tooth" was never meant to be a justification for excessive violence. It started out as a law *limiting* violence—take *no more than* a tooth for a tooth—because people were ready and willing to kill someone over a broken tooth. Jesus put a stop to that. To return violence for violence only continues its cycle, and it justifies violence instead of nonviolence when settling conflicts.

- Why is the command "Love your enemies" hard to follow?
- Why is our culture so familiar with methods of violence, yet so ignorant of methods of nonviolent conflict resolution?
- What do you think might end the cycle of violence?
- If someone is angry and wishes to do physical harm to you, what are your nonviolent options?
- When it comes to choosing between violent and nonviolent methods, does gender make any difference? If so, why? If not, why not?

For Children

An old rule used to tell people that if someone knocked out your tooth, than you should be able to knock out that person's tooth. Jesus said that this old rule is wrong. If someone hits you, you should not hit back.

- Why do you think Jesus got rid of that old rule?
- What usually starts fights on the playground?
- What usually causes fights to keep going on?
- What is the best way to stop a fight?

Closing

Brush them and floss them and take them to the dentist, and they will stay with you. Ignore them and they'll go away. —American Dental Association

(Success Every Day)

Eighth Sunday of the Year

The readings for this Sunday do not occur in 1999, 2002, or 2005.

Trust in God

Scripture

- *Isaiah 49:14–15.* God is like a woman nursing a child of her own womb. She would not forget her child, and God would not forget us.
- *1 Corinthians 4:1–5.* We must not judge others; only God, who sees all things and knows all things, can be a judge.
- *Matthew 6:24–34.* Do not worry unnecessarily about the type of food you will eat and the type of clothes you must wear. God will take care of your basic needs.

Theme

Trust God. God will not forget us. God will not judge us harshly or unfairly. God will provide for us what we need. We do not need to be overly anxious about things that are not very important. We are more significant than the lilies of the field, yet they are beautiful. If God takes such good care of the field, we can be sure that God will take good care of us.

Focusing Object

Flowers

Reflections

This passage is often accused of justifying laziness—"Why should I do anything? The flowers in the field don't do any work, so why should I? God will provide. I must not worry."

• Why is this a distortion of the meaning of the Gospel?

Against the direct advice of Jesus as stated in this passage, we have become a people obsessed with clothes and food. People overeat and become obese, people starve themselves in order to imitate the emaciated models they see in ads (whose bodies are often computer enhanced!), and people kill one another in order to steal designer jackets and shoes.

• How did we become this way?
• What contributes to this situation?
• What can you do to help reverse this cycle?

By focusing on the unnecessary, we sometimes neglect the necessary. A rise in materialism and consumer-economy interests takes place at the expense of nature and environmental concerns.

• What happens to the earth's environment when human beings focus mainly on making money, selling products, and creating advertising campaigns?
• Is the quality of the earth's natural resources important to you? What can be done to turn the culture's attention to the needs of Planet Earth?

For Teenagers

Jesus tells us to look to the flowers. They are beautiful just as they are, even though they are not concerned with designer clothes and are not obsessed with overeating or dieting.

Magazine ads and TV commercials do their best to convince us that a person becomes more popular, more intelligent, more successful, and better looking if he or she wears their brand of clothing or uses their skin and hair products.

Fast food was first created to serve a need—it was a convenient way to feed people who were too busy to prepare quality meals for themselves. Fast food generally isn't very healthy or nutritious, and it was never meant to be a substitute for home-cooked meals, but because of advertising it has become the food of choice for some people. Many children would rather eat out at a fast-food place than eat quality home cooking at their own dinner table!

- Why are many teenagers willing to be brainwashed into believing obviously false advertising?
- How can teenagers see what is true when much time and money are spent promoting what is false?

Flowers need a balanced ecology in order to thrive. God has done a wonderful job of creating the earth, but human beings have sometimes done a poor job as stewards. When we pay more attention to advertising and products and having "the right look," we end up neglecting things that really matter. Many factories and industries are hurting the environment.

- The environment has no voice of its own. How can you be its voice?
- How are consumerism and materialism related to the destruction of the planet? How are teenagers partially responsible?

For Children

Jesus tells us not to worry about what to wear and what to eat. He tells us to look at the flowers that grow outside. They are so beautiful, yet they don't worry about what they eat or how they look. God gives them rain and dirt and sunshine so they can grow and look pretty.

- Have you ever planted flowers? If so, did you plant them outside or inside?
- What do flowers get planted in?
- If you plant flowers inside, do you have to water them more or less than flowers planted outside? Why?

- Does God care for you as much as you would care for a flower? How does God show us God's care?

Closing

The earth belongs as much
to those who are to come after us . . .
as to us;
and we have no right,
by anything we do or neglect,
to involve them
in unnecessary penalties, or
deprive them of benefits.

—John Ruskin
(Action 2000: C Cycle)

Ninth Sunday of the Year

The readings for this Sunday do not occur in 1999, 2002, or 2005.

Faith in God's Word

Scripture

- *Deuteronomy 11:18,26–28.* Moses warns the people to take God's word into their mind and soul; obedience will bring a blessing, disobedience will bring a curse.
- *Romans 3:21–25,28.* Paul explains that all of us have sinned, and so none of us can *earn* redemption. It is a gift that we receive through faith.
- *Matthew 7:21–27.* Jesus warns that those who enter heaven will be those who do God's will—those who build their house on a solid foundation of rock. Those who merely call out, "Lord, Lord," but do not live out God's will are building on sand.

Theme

Moses wants God's word to be a foundation for everything the people do. That foundation must be rock solid, not shifting like the sands. Only a fool would build on sand. True believers will have faith in God's way, shown to us by Jesus, even though they still falter and sin.

Focusing Object
A rock and a container of sand

Reflections

For Adults

Fools build their house on shifting sand. Only the wise understand the need for a rock-solid foundation.

- What are the rock-solid foundations on which you have built your life?
- When you were younger, did you find that you had counted on some things that had turned out to be shifting sand? What went wrong? How did you discover that such a foundation would not support your life?

A person with integrity does the right thing because it is right; it doesn't matter if anyone is looking or not. A person with integrity doesn't speak empty words or make empty promises; his or her life actions reflect the commitment of those words and promises.

- Name a person of integrity. Why do you consider him or her to be a person of integrity?

For Teenagers

Many young people invest a lot of energy in building their life on the shifting sand of fads. They are encouraged to do so because the business world enjoys making money off their insecurities. So billboards, magazine ads, and TV commercials easily convince them to buy things they don't really need, in order to be "attractive, successful, and happy."

- What are some of the most widely bought labels and designer brands? Why do teenagers continue to fall for the tricks of advertising? Why are they so easy to fool?
- What would be a wiser response to advertising? How else can teenagers invest their time, money, and energy? If they didn't spend money on designer jeans and shoes, hair and skin products, and other luxuries that they don't really need, how might the world be a better place? How would each individual teenager be better off?

- The world is full of fools. But the world is also full of wise persons. Who in your opinion is a wise person—a person whose word means something; who has integrity; whom you can trust to do the right thing, even when no one is looking? Describe someone you know who is such a person, and tell what makes that person wise.
- Can you fake integrity? Can you fake wisdom? If a person tried to do so, how long do you think it could last? How easy is it to fool everyone?

For Children

Jesus says that only a fool would build a house on sand. A wise person would build a house on a solid rock foundation.

- If you wanted to make a tall tower with some building blocks, where would be the best place to build it—on a pile of sand or on something more solid, like the sidewalk? Why? What would happen if you tried to stack blocks on top of a pile of sand?
- What would happen if someone built an entire house on sand? Do you think it would fall down or stay up? Why?
- Jesus wants us to be wise and not foolish. Name some of the wise things that you do. Name some of the foolish things that you do.

Closing

It is true that you may fool all the people some of the time; you can even fool some of the people all the time; but you can't fool all of the people all the time. —Abraham Lincoln

(Familiar Quotations)

Tenth Sunday of the Year

The readings for this Sunday do not occur in 1999.

9 June 2002
5 June 2005

Healing
with Mercy

Scripture

- *Hosea 6:3–6.* God wants to be known and loved by us; God does not desire empty sacrifices or burnt offerings.
- *Romans 4:18–25.* Abraham and Sarah believe in God, who promises them a child in their later years. We must have similar faith in God.
- *Matthew 9:9–13.* Jesus comes to Matthew, who is working in his tax office. Matthew leaves everything behind and follows. Later Jesus is criticized for socializing with sinners such as tax collectors. Jesus quotes the Hebrew Scriptures, and says that the physician can help those who know they are sick, not those who are sick but think they are well.

Theme

The first reading is quoted in the Gospel—God does not want sacrifice but mercy—and Jesus asks those criticizing his choice of friends to study the meaning of that. Although Matthew is a tax collector (a group who are noted for their corruption), he leaves behind all his figures and paperwork and immediately follows Jesus. We need to model the faith of Matthew, Abraham, and Sarah—to know when we need God's help and to trust in God's mercy and care.

Focusing Object
A small pad of paper and a pencil, or a calculator

Reflections

For Adults

Jesus comes to heal the sick, not the well. Of course, we are all sinners so we are all sick and broken, and we are all in need of Jesus. Some claim that the church should not admit sinners like Matthew. But Jesus welcomes them. The church should be where we gather to forgive one another and to strengthen one another's faith.

- Do you find Sunday worship to be a place where your faith is made stronger and your sinfulness is forgiven? If so, how?
- God wants mercy and love, not empty sacrifice and rituals. Does any part of your worship seem to be an empty ritual? If so, how do you contribute to that emptiness? How can you enrich your worship so that it does not seem so empty?
- Where in your life do you observe mercy, forgiveness, and love? Is your family such a place? your circle of friends? your workplace? If so, how?
- Where in your life have you demonstrated mercy, forgiveness, and love?
- Almost every major action and decision we make are observed by others. Do you see yourself as a potential model of Christianity? What might younger observers think of your actions?

For Teenagers

Matthew is in his tax office, probably adding up figures or examining his accounts. He is occupied with the math of his business, his lifework. Jesus walks in and simply says, "Follow me." Immediately Matthew obeys. He leaves his calculations on the desk and never returns.

- Why would someone just get up and go like that? Why would someone leave all their work behind? Do you think Jesus is that compelling with his two-word invitation? Do you think that Matthew doesn't enjoy his work anyway?

- When you are doing your homework, how focused are you? If someone came in and said, "Follow me," would you dump your notebook, pencil, and calculator and get up and go? Would you finish your current problem first? Would your reaction depend on who asked? Would it depend on when your assignment was due? How would you respond if you were put in Matthew's situation?

Jesus is criticized for eating with sinners and outcasts. He has unpopular people as friends. Jesus answers this by saying that only the sick need a doctor, and that he has come to call sinners, not righteous people.

- How would you respond if someone very popular came by and insulted you for sitting with unpopular people? What would you think or say or do if someone who is popular called your friends losers? Would it make much difference if many people were watching you and waiting to see how you would respond? Why or why not?
- What do you think Jesus means by his comment about the sick, not the well, needing a doctor?
- How do you think Matthew and the other social outcasts feel about being called outcasts and sinners? How do you think they feel after Jesus' response?

For Children

Matthew is working in his office when Jesus comes in. Matthew is probably adding up numbers at the time. Jesus says two words: "Follow me." Matthew leaves all his work behind and follows Jesus right out the door.

- Do you think Matthew knows who Jesus is? Why or why not?
- Do you think Matthew is surprised to have Jesus come in and ask him to follow? Why or why not?
- If Matthew was your age, do you think he would have asked his mother or father for permission to go with Jesus? Why or why not?
- What would you have done if you were Matthew?

Closing

Be careful how you live;
you may be the only Bible
some person ever reads.
—W. J. Toms

(Vision 2000: A Cycle)

Eleventh Sunday
of the Year

13 June 1999
16 June 2002
12 June 2005

Laborers for the Harvest

Scripture

- *Exodus 19:2–6.* God bears the people of Israel on eagles' wings and keeps them safe. God tells Moses that if the people keep the Covenant, they shall be a holy people.
- *Romans 5:6–11.* Paul explains that although it might be reasonable for a very good person to consider dying for a righteous person, it would not be reasonable to die for a sinner. Yet that is exactly what Jesus did for us.
- *Matthew 9:36—10:8.* Jesus sees that the harvest is plentiful but the laborers are few. He gives the twelve Apostles authority to travel and preach and heal.

Theme

We have a rich history of God's love acting in our lives. Moses is asked to remind the wandering Israelites that God cares for and protects those who keep the Covenant. Paul reminds us that what Jesus did for us was an incredible act of love. Matthew reports that the Apostles were commissioned to heal the sick, raise the dead, cleanse lepers, and cast out demons without payment. In the world today, the harvest is still plentiful. Are there enough laborers?

Focusing Object

A gardening tool

Reflections

For Adults

God's love has been abundant in our lives. Moses, Paul, and Matthew all want us to be aware of that.
- How has God's love been abundant in your life?
- How have you given back to God without thought of being paid?

Jesus started out his ministry with twelve laborers to attend to the plentiful harvest. It seemed like impossible odds—Jesus plus twelve, to deal with a world of people.
- Who are some laborers you know that have ministered to God's abundant harvest?
- How have you been a laborer for God's harvest?
- How are the odds of successful harvesting better now than they were when Jesus had only twelve helpers?
- How were the odds of success better in Jesus' time?
- If you think a life of harvesting for God is impossible, what do you see as the biggest obstacles? If you think it is possible, what do you see as the biggest helps?

For Teenagers

God's love has been abundant in our lives. Moses, Paul, and Matthew all want us to be aware of that.
- How has God's love been abundant in your life?
- How have you given back to God without thought of being paid?

Jesus asked twelve inexperienced, uneducated people to travel all over the countryside preaching, healing, and spreading the good news about God's love. It must have seemed like an impossible task.
- Would you have gone along with this plan if you had been alive during those days and had been invited to be an apostle? Why or why not?

- What are some ways of spreading the good news about God's love that are available to us today but were not available to the original twelve Apostles two thousand years ago?
- Which task seems more impossible—for the twelve Apostles to go out and preach and heal and bring people back to God's way, or for today's church members to go out and preach and heal and bring a modern people back to God's way? Explain your answer.

For Children

Jesus wants us to talk about him and to help other people to know Jesus and love him. He says that doing so is like taking your gardening tools and going out into your garden to get all the vegetables and fruits that are ready to be cut down and brought in.

- Do you ever talk to anyone about Jesus? If so, whom?
- Have you ever grown any fruits or vegetables? How long do you have to wait before they are ripe and ready to be picked? How do you know when they are ready?
- Have you ever gone to a store to pick out fruit or vegetables? How do you know which ones are ripe? What color is a ripe tomato? What color is a tomato that isn't ripe yet? What color is a ripe banana? What color is a banana that isn't ripe yet? What color is a banana that is too ripe? When a fruit or vegetable gets more and more ripe, does it get harder or softer?
- Do you think people have to get "ripe" in order to hear God's word?

Closing

You must act as if it is impossible to fail. —An Ashanti proverb

(Acts of Faith)

Twelfth Sunday of the Year

20 June 1999
23 June 2002
19 June 2005

Cherished by God

Scripture

- *Jeremiah 20:10–13.* God sees the heart and mind of those trying to do good; God will deliver the needy from evildoers.
- *Romans 5:12–15.* Many have died since sin came into the world, but many more are now given grace because of Jesus Christ.
- *Matthew 10:26–33.* God watches the sparrows and helps them to fly without falling, yet the value of God's human family is greater than that of sparrows. The truth of God's way must be proclaimed without fear. Do not fear those who can hurt the body; fear those who can hurt the soul.

Theme

We are important to God. Even the hairs on our head are counted and known by God. Jeremiah, in all his turmoil, knows this. Paul, who is imprisoned for his faith, knows this. Jesus urges us not only to know this but to shout it from the rooftops. Our life will be more peaceful if we fully know and accept God's providence.

Focusing Object

A bird

Reflections

We are important to God. Even when others are questioning our significance, attacking our motives, or criticizing our abilities, we need to remember that we are important to God.

- When have you felt completely rejected and defeated? What happened? How did you gain strength to get yourself through that part of your life?
- How does your knowledge of God's care for you make a difference in your everyday life?

Jesus urges us to take the truths that are whispered in the dark and to proclaim them from the rooftops in the light of day. Jesus asks us to be unafraid of those who can hurt only our body and to worry only about what can hurt our soul.

- What truths are you generally afraid to talk about because of the controversy doing so may cause? What would Jesus say about that?
- When it comes to controversy, what are people generally afraid of?

God cherishes even the sparrows, who cannot fly without God's help. Yet sparrows are worth nothing compared with us.

- Is it easy or difficult to believe that you are cherished by God? How so?
- Is it easy or difficult to believe in yourself? Do you think you are significant? Why or why not?
- Do you think most people your age feel their worth from their friends' opinions of them or from their own opinions about themselves? Explain your answer.
- Who else cherishes you? Who believes in you? Who knows you are significant?

Jesus tells us to proclaim the truth from the rooftops. Jesus urges us to not be afraid of anyone who can only hurt our body, but to fear whatever can hurt our soul.

- What can hurt your soul? What influences from today's world can prevent you from being the best you can be? How do you counteract those influences?
- What things are you afraid to talk about because you may be teased or mocked? How often do you talk about your inner fears and concerns? How often do you talk about your biggest dreams for yourself and for the world? What is the most important focus of your life right now?

For Children

Jesus tells us that even sparrows—tiny little birds— are important to God. They can't fly without God's help. Yet God holds them up as they glide through the sky without falling. Jesus also tells us that we are more important to God than the sparrows.

- Have you ever watched birds fly? How do they do it? What do they do with their wings?
- Have you ever fed any birds? Have you ever watched birds eat from a bird feeder or from the ground?
- Do you think birds are important to God?
- Do you think you are more important to God than birds? Why or why not? What do you think are some of God's favorite things about you?
- What are your favorite things about yourself?
- Who are some people that think you are important?

Closing

No one can make you feel inferior without your consent. —Eleanor Roosevelt

(The Promise of a New Day)

Thirteenth Sunday of the Year

27 June 1999
30 June 2002
26 June 2005

Service

Scripture

- *2 Kings 4:8–11,14–16.* Elisha the Prophet is treated with hospitality and care when he visits the Shunemite woman and her husband. Elisha promises her that she will have a son within a year.
- *Romans 6:3–4,8–11.* Paul reminds the Romans that Christ was raised to new life, and so by being baptized, they are now part of Jesus' death and Resurrection. They must see themselves as dead to sin and alive with the spirit of Jesus.
- *Matthew 10:37–42.* Jesus says that whoever welcomes a prophet will receive a reward; whoever gives even a cup of water to a disciple will also receive a reward.

Theme

Being baptized into the death and life of Jesus means living for Jesus, following Jesus, and being a disciple of Jesus'. Welcoming such disciples, as well as prophets and holy people, will bring a reward. Anything we can do—even just giving a cup of cold water—is an act of service that will be appreciated.

Focusing Object
A cup of cold water

Reflections

Sometimes we think of choosing a life of service as being some big, grand life decision that calls us to exotic missionary places and takes us away from all things familiar. But anyone, anywhere can live a life of service simply by observing what people need and being attentive to those needs.

- When did someone notice you were thirsty and offer you a cup of cold water or some other drink? How did you appreciate that small gesture?
- When did you notice someone who needed something, and offer it instead of waiting for that person to ask for it?
- Do you think these small gestures of noticing someone's need and trying to take care of it are unusual these days, or do you think they are common? How so?

In today's readings Jesus is speaking primarily of hospitality to prophets, holy people, and lowly ones who are disciples.

- Who is a holy person that you know? Who is a modern prophet? Do you know any "lowly disciples"?
- Why would Jesus isolate only these types of people? Is he being elitist? Do you think he only wants us to serve holy people, disciples, and prophets because other types of people are not worthy of our hospitality or attention? Why or why not?

In today's Gospel Jesus talks to us about service.

- If Jesus appeared to you in the flesh and asked you to be a special disciple, what do you imagine that might entail?
- How do you picture "big-time" service—living in the inner city? volunteering at a shelter? spending a week in Appalachia? going to South America for a summer? or joining a missionary order and spending the rest of your life in Africa?

- How do you picture "ordinary" service? Give some examples.

Some jobs have great potential for simple human service, for example, smiling and being extra friendly as you bag groceries, looking out for what the children may need as you baby-sit, noticing whose coffee cup is empty as you wait tables, or being sure the newspapers you deliver are always placed close to your customers' door.

- What are some simple things that you might do every day that can be compared to giving someone a cup of cold water?
- What kind of reward do you think comes to someone who serves another?

For Children

Jesus tells us that giving someone even just a cup of cold water is a good thing.

- When was the last time you can remember being really thirsty? Why were you so thirsty? What happened? How did it feel when you finally got a drink of water?
- Do you think Jesus only wants us to help one another out by giving cups of cold water, or would he like us to help in some other ways? Can you think of some other ways?

Closing

The only ones among you who will be really happy are those who have sought and found a way to serve. —Albert Schweitzer

(Vision 2000: A Cycle)

Fourteenth Sunday of the Year

4 July 1999
7 July 2002
3 July 2005

The Yoke
of Jesus

Scripture

- *Zechariah 9:9–10.* The meek Savior of Jerusalem shall come riding on the foal of a donkey, not in a chariot and not with a warrior's weapon. Peace shall be proclaimed to all nations.
- *Romans 8:9,11–13.* The Spirit of God dwells in all, and all must live by the Spirit. With death, bodies will come back to life.
- *Matthew 11:25–30.* God reveals to children that which is hidden from the clever and the learned. Jesus calls the people to come to him for refreshment when tired and burdened, for the yoke of Jesus is easy and the burden is light.

Theme

Zechariah the Prophet speaks of a meek savior coming to proclaim peace, without the aid of any weapons of war. Jesus is that gentle Savior who confuses the sophisticated and delights the children. The yoke of Jesus is bearable to those who learn from his humble heart—those who live by the Spirit. Even pain is easier to bear when we know the ways of Jesus.

Focusing Object
A baby blanket

Reflections

For Adults

Life is not easy. Everyone suffers and has to deal with problems. But we are here because those who came before us suffered through life, dealt with their problems, and did what they could to pass life on to the rest of us. We can do the same for those who come after us. When we are most burdened, it is comforting to know that our ancestors dealt with suffering, and so can we. The pain is eased.

- Taking Jesus' yoke upon your shoulders doesn't mean the pain won't exist; it just means that it will be bearable. How does it ease the pain in your life to know that Jesus went before you, and that Jesus goes with you now?
- Who do you look to when you need a courageous example of how to deal with the suffering and disappointments of life? When have you needed that person's example to help you bear with pain?

Children often don't understand pain. But they suffer through it, and those who are fortunate are comforted by caring adults who hold them, rock them, sing to them, and love them.

- What can we learn from children when it comes to dealing with pain?
- What can we learn from children when it comes to bringing peace to the world?

For Teenagers

According to Jesus children know more about some of God's secrets than do the most clever adults.

- Have you ever held a crying baby? Have you seen anyone else do it? Can anything be done to stop a baby's crying? When the baby finally stops crying, is it because the pain has gone away? How can rocking, singing, and cuddling help?

As we grow older, we perhaps don't cry when we skin our knees or drop our toys, but we still have plenty of pain in our life. We never outgrow the ability to hurt or the need for comfort.

- What might be one of God's secrets about dealing with suffering or about comforting someone in pain?

Jesus doesn't promise us a life without pain, but he says that the yoke and burden will be light and easy to bear.

- When have you had to deal with great physical pain? What happened?
- When have you had to deal with great emotional pain? What happened?
- Which is easier to deal with—physical pain or emotional pain? Why?
- How does living in the spirit of Jesus affect the way we deal with our pain?

For Children

Jesus tells us that if we make him a special part of our life, then life will be better for us.

- Is Jesus a special part of your life? If so, how?
- How can knowing about Jesus make someone's life better?
- Do you know any adults who ask Jesus to help them get through the tough times in their life? If so, who are they?

Closing

If we stand tall, it is because we stand on the backs of those who came before us. —A Yoruba proverb

(Acts of Faith)

Fifteenth Sunday of the Year

11 July 1999
14 July 2002
10 July 2005

God's Word Yields Fruit

Scripture

- *Isaiah 55:10–11.* God's word is fruitful, just as the sown seed with the rain and sun is fruitful.
- *Romans 8:18–23.* The suffering of today seems unimportant compared with the glory of God that is yet to be shown to us. Groaning and agony are part of any stage of growth, internal or external.
- *Matthew 13:1–23.* The word of God is like the seed sown by a farmer. Much of it runs into peril and does not become fruitful, yet some of it lands on good soil and yields a great amount of grain.

Theme

Any kind of growth is difficult. As we grow, we suffer and we learn. As seeds grow, they have to break open for shoots to form. Then, during their struggle, they can be choked, trampled on, or dried out before they actually become grain to be harvested. Although difficult, growth does happen— it happens with seeds, with people, and with the word of God.

Focusing Object
Seeds in a jar, packet, or dish

Reflections

In the parable of the sower and the seed, we can be the ground the seed falls upon.

- When are you like the footpath, where the seed gets eaten up by a bird? When you don't listen to the word, is it because you don't understand it or because some interruption or life detail takes your attention away from it? How so?
- When are you like the rock where the seed dries out? When you don't listen to the word, is it because, although you did hear it once, the suffering of a life crisis has caused you to falter? How so?
- When are you like the ground with the thorns that choke off the seed? When you don't listen to the word, is it because so many other voices—money, status, power, and the like—are so much louder? How so?
- When are you like the good soil? When you do listen to the word, what other factors in your life help to make you fertile and ready to accept the seed so that it can grow?

In the parable of the sower and the seed, we can be the sower as well.

- What seeds of God's word do you plant? What might happen to those seeds? What has already happened to them?
- Is it frustrating to be the sower, without much control over how the seeds may grow? Or do you trust that seeds, which are meant to grow, will somehow grow no matter what?

This farmer who is sowing doesn't seem to have much of a plan. There isn't an organized effort to prepare all the soil so that none of the seed is wasted. It's just thrown all over the place, with the hope that some of it will fall on good soil and grow.

- Do you think that is a good strategy for a farmer whose life depends upon successfully growing things? Why or why not?

- Why do you think God throws out seed to bad soil as well as to good soil?
- If our job is to spread the message of God, should we have a plan that is more dependable than this farmer's plan? Why or why not? What might such a plan look like?

Even if we are very deliberate about where we "sow the seeds" of God's message, we can't always control how people will receive it.

- Do you think it is better to aim for just the good soil, so that we mainly bring the message to people who are ready to listen to it? Why or why not?
- Do you think it is better to spend some time working the soil, so that dry, rocky, or thorny areas might become more fertile and ready to accept the seed? Why or why not?

Not only are we asked to bring the seed of God's word to others, also we are asked to receive the seed of God's word from others.

- When do you feel like the good soil, fertile and waiting for God's word to come to you and bring you new life?
- When do you feel like dry, rocky, or thorny soil, not ready for God's word to grow within you?

For Children

The farmer throws the seeds into the field—some of them grow and some of them don't. Jesus teaches us about life—some of us listen and some of us don't.

- How is the farmer in the Gospel story like Jesus?
- Have you ever planted seeds? If so, did you plant them in a special place, or did you throw them all over in different places?
- What could you do to the ground first, before you plant the seeds, to make the ground ready for the seeds and to help the seeds grow in the best way?

Closing

Sow a thought, and you reap an act;
Sow an act, and you reap a habit;
Sow a habit, and you reap a character;
Sow a character; and you reap a destiny.
—Samuel Smiles
(Days of Healing, Days of Joy)

Sixteenth Sunday of the Year

18 July 1999
21 July 2002
17 July 2005

God's Universal Care

Scripture

- *Wisdom 12:13,16–19.* Although powerful and just, God is also caring and merciful, giving us hope that sins will be forgiven.
- *Romans 8:26–27.* The people in the church of Rome are assured that the Spirit will help them to pray—and will even pray for them. It is all right if they cannot find the right words, God knows what is in their hearts.
- *Matthew 13:24–43.* God is like the farmer who allows the weeds to grow with the wheat. God is like the woman who kneads a tiny amount of yeast into the bread dough, and the whole loaf rises. God has the power of the tiniest mustard seed that grows into the large shrub where all the birds come to live.

Theme

God knows what is in our heart. God understands. God forgives. God allows sinners and saints to live together and grow together right up to harvest time. It is too hard for us to separate the weeds from the wheat without hurting the wheat. It's not our job. Let's allow God to do it.

Focusing Object

A shaft of wheat and a weed

Reflections

For Adults

No one is perfect. Everyone makes mistakes. That's why it is God's job to separate the weeds from the wheat. But it is our job to become wheat and not a weed.

- Is it possible for us to separate the weeds from the wheat? Can we always know who the saints and the sinners are in the world?
- Have you ever gotten a terrible first impression of a person, only to realize later that this person you judged poorly is actually wonderful? If so, what happened to change your mind?
- If a survey were taken of the people you work with, would most of them cast you as a weed or as wheat? Why do you think so? What would be said about you?

Any seed that grows into a plant is rather small—whether it becomes a weed, a shaft of wheat, or a mustard shrub. The amount of yeast mixed into bread dough is also very small, but it affects the whole loaf.

- Your influence on the world may seem small, but it is significant. Where do you have an influence (even the tiniest amount) on making this world more like the place Jesus would want it to be?

For Teenagers

It's lucky for us that God is the only one who distinguishes the weeds from the wheat.

- Think of your teachers at school. Would all of them completely agree on whether you should be characterized as a weed or as wheat? If so, what would they say? If not, how might they disagree? What would the "wheat voters" say about you? What would the "weed voters" say about you? Do you think any of the wheat voters might convince the others of your good qualities? Or do you think it would be more likely that the weed voters would be the convincing ones? Why?

- Think of a person you might consider to be a weed. Can you see any positive characteristics in that person? If you concentrated on those positives for a whole month, do you think your opinion of this person might change? Why or why not?
- Do you know anyone who is perfectly good, perfectly wonderful all the time? Do you know anyone who isn't perfect but who could be called saintly? Describe why you see this person in this way. Would anyone disagree with your opinion? If so, why?

For Children

Weeds that grow near plants can sometimes take over the ground so much that the plants die. That's why a lot of farmers and gardeners don't like weeds.

- Have you ever seen weeds in a garden or a field? What do they look like?

Jesus says that the bad weeds and the good wheat must grow up together and not be separated while they are growing. He said that you might hurt some of the good wheat as you try to get rid of the bad weeds while both are growing. And sometimes you can't always tell the weeds from the wheat.

- Can people sometimes be like weeds and wheat? How?
- Sometimes nice people do bad things, and sometimes people who have done bad things can be nice. Is it easy or hard to figure out whom you want as your friends?

Closing

There is so much good in the worst of us,
And so much bad in the best of us,
That it hardly behooves any of us
To talk about the rest of us.

—Governor Edward Wallis Hoch
(Kansas), 1849–1925
(Familiar Quotations)

Seventeenth Sunday of the Year

25 July 1999
28 July 2002
24 July 2005

The Reign of God

Scripture

- *1 Kings 3:5, 7–12.* When God asks Solomon what he would most want, Solomon doesn't ask for riches, power, or long life, but requests an understanding heart that can judge right and wrong. God promises Solomon that no one will be his equal.
- *Romans 8:28–30.* God makes all things work out for those who love God and try to do the right thing.
- *Matthew 13:44–52.* Jesus tells a parable about the Reign of God. He says it is like a field with a buried treasure or like a priceless pearl, worth everything a person owns. It is also like a dragnet that is thrown into a lake and collects everything, so that later the useless can be thrown away and the worthwhile kept.

Theme

The Reign of God is both delightful and frightening. It is delightful to come across a treasure buried in a field or a perfect pearl. For such a precious commodity, we might invest our life savings. However, the image of everything being divided into the "useless" and the "worthwhile" is rather frightening.

Focusing Object
Pearls or a toy necklace

Reflections

For Adults

Being wise means having the ability to recognize what is of real value.

- Where in your life have you found value that might be unrecognizable by our materialistic culture?

Obviously the fullness of the Reign of God exists in heaven, but its beginnings also exist on earth.

- Where have you caught a glimpse of the Reign of God—when have you sensed a bit of "heaven on earth"?
- If more people worried less about their own treasures and more about the treasures of the Reign of God, they would find themselves all the richer—do you truly believe that? Explain your answer.

The image of being dragged in by a net with all the garbage of the earth and then being judged by God and the angels as to whether you are useless or worthwhile is not pleasant.

- Why do you think Jesus uses images like this to describe the last judgment if he also wants us to know and believe in a loving, merciful God?
- Do you believe that any human being created by God's own divine hand could be judged useless at the end of time? Why or why not?

For Teenagers

The Reign (power and control) of God is also known as the Kingdom of Heaven. It takes place on earth and reaches its fullness in heaven.

- Often in school, business, politics, and even social settings people try to assert their own power and take control of things. Where have you seen this happen?

When people surrender their life to God's power, life is different. Then people don't try to control things or one another; they try to work together so that God's way rules. This rarely occurs on earth, but it happens once in a while. There is peace, understanding, and cooperation, and no fear, competition, or dishonesty.

- Have you ever seen this happen? If so, where? What was the situation?
- Do you think you can do anything to help bring forth the Reign of God—at home, at school, at your job, with your friends? Why or why not? What would have to happen to create a little heaven on earth?

For Children

Jesus says that heaven is better than the best treasure and better than the most perfect pearl necklace.

- What is the best treasure you can imagine? Why do people like necklaces so much?

Life on earth could be almost as wonderful as life in heaven if everyone tried to act like Jesus.

- What would it be like if everyone tried to act like Jesus? In what ways do you already try to do that?

Closing

Help another's boat across, and lo!
Thine own has reached the shore!
—An old Hindu proverb
(Vision 2000: A Cycle)

Eighteenth Sunday of the Year

1 August 1999
4 August 2002
31 July 2005

Feeding the Hungry

Scripture

- *Isaiah 55:1–3.* The prophet welcomes all who are thirsty, hungry, and poor to come and drink, eat, and not worry about the cost. God is bountiful.
- *Romans 8:35,37–39.* Absolutely, positively nothing can or will ever separate people from the love of Jesus, the Christ.
- *Matthew 14:13–21.* Jesus is with a crowd of five thousand people, not counting the women and children. No shops are nearby for people to buy food, and the disciples have only five loaves of bread and two fish. But all the people eat well, and their leftovers fill twelve baskets.

Theme

Food and drink are always significant to people who are hungry and thirsty. That is why Isaiah uses those images when describing God's bounty. That is why Jesus insists to the disciples that the crowd be fed. Jesus tries to withdraw from people, but he is overcome with pity when he sees them waiting for him as he steps off of the boat. Jesus' love is great—we will never be separated from it.

Focusing Object

A basket of leftover bread pieces

Reflections

The phrase "not counting the women and children" is most significant because in the days of Jesus, women and children literally did not count for anything. They were property of their husbands, and they had no rights. Yet it was (and sometimes still is) the women who took care of both the children and the men, thinking ahead to plan for meals and other needs. Many Scripture scholars propose the likelihood that the women in this group have thought ahead and indeed have brought some food along for their journey. Once they are sitting down together, it is quite possible that they begin to trust one another more. Once they trust one another, they start sharing the food they have, and all this food just seems to come from nowhere. Perhaps the miracle is not one of increasing the feeding potential of the five loaves and two fish but one of increasing the feeding potential of the people themselves.

- Which do you think would be the greater or more amazing miracle: that Jesus would be able to increase the size and abundance of the actual food items the disciples found, or that Jesus would be able to encourage the generous nature of the people gathered so that they felt comfortable sharing their food with strangers?
- How comfortable would you feel taking out food you brought for your family in the middle of a hungry crowd?

Before distributing the loaves and fish, Jesus looked up to heaven, blessed and broke them, and gave the food to his disciples.

- This wording sounds like the description of the Last Supper. The Gospel writer appears to be making a connection between the feeding of the crowd and the feeding of those at the Last Supper. Why is this significant?

Before Jesus meets up with this crowd, he is actually trying to get away and be by himself, because he has just heard about the death of John the Baptizer. But as soon as his boat reaches the shore, thousands of people are waiting there for him.

- What do you think Jesus' immediate thoughts are upon seeing this huge crowd?
- Why do you think the disciples suggest to him that he make all the people go away to find something to eat?
- Why do you think Jesus insists that the crowds be fed and not be turned away?

The disciples start with only five loaves and two fish. Five thousand people are there, not counting the women and children. Yet everyone eats their fill, and the leftovers fill twelve baskets.

- What is your attitude about leftovers? Do you see leftovers as an aged meal whose flavors have had more time to blend and improve? Or do you see leftovers as food that should have been thrown away?
- If you were poor and hadn't eaten a meal for two days, would your attitude toward leftovers be different? If so, how?

For Children

A really big crowd of people gather around Jesus. It is suppertime, and everyone is hungry. Jesus' friends don't have much food for themselves—only five loaves of bread and two fish. And they don't want to share their food with all those other people because they are hungry too!

- What do you think Jesus' friends first say when Jesus tells them to feed the crowds of people with their own food? What would you have said if you had been told to share your supper with thousands of people?

- When everyone is finished eating, there are actually leftovers—twelve baskets full. More food is left over than what Jesus' friends started with! Yet everyone ate until they were full. What do you think Jesus' friends say when they see that?
- Do you like eating leftovers? Why or why not?

Closing

If God were to appear to starving people, he wouldn't dare appear in any form other than food. —Mohandas Gandhi

(Action 2000: C Cycle)

Nineteenth Sunday of the Year

8 August 1999
11 August 2002
7 August 2005

Peter's Faith in Jesus

Scripture

- *1 Kings 19:9,11–13.* Elijah is told that Yahweh will be passing by the cave where Elijah is sheltered. Wind, earthquake, and fire all occur, but it is in a quiet whispering sound that Elijah knows of Yahweh's presence.
- *Romans 9:1–5.* Paul feels deep sorrow that all his Jewish brothers and sisters cannot accept Jesus Christ, another Jew, as the Messiah.
- *Matthew 14:22–33.* In the middle of a storm, Jesus, walking on the water, comes to the disciples' boat and calls Peter to come out to him.

Theme

God is always present to us, always with us. Elijah recognizes Yahweh's presence, even though it is subtle. The disciples, especially Peter, are eager to believe that Jesus is with them, despite the unbelievable circumstances. Paul's sorrow that everyone is not being moved by the Holy Spirit to know the truth could echo our own modern-day concern that violence is becoming more widespread and that goodness seems to be old-fashioned. Yet we know that God is always present, always with us.

Focusing Object

A boat

Reflections

Peter believes in Jesus, yet Peter is afraid when he realizes the danger of what he is doing—actually walking on water in the middle of the lake, in the middle of a storm. His faith is not strong enough to calm his fear, but it is strong enough to direct him to the One who will give him any help he needs—Jesus.

- When was your faith strong enough to direct you to ask Jesus for help, even though it wasn't strong enough to eliminate your fear?
- Do you think we can ever have faith so strong that we never fear? Would that be a good thing or not? How would that affect our decision making? A boat is often used as a symbol of the church.

It is easy to picture the church today caught in the middle of a storm of uncertainty, reaching out to Jesus for help.

- Who are the Peters of our time, brave enough to take the risk and go the extra step toward Jesus, despite their fear and confusion?
- What would Jesus say to us in the church about our faith and courage?

For Teenagers

Peter takes a big risk. Trusting Jesus, he steps out onto the lake in the middle of a storm. But when the wind frightens him, he begins to sink. Jesus is disappointed that Peter's faith isn't greater.

- When did you ever take a big risk because you trusted someone? Did it work out, or did you get into trouble?
- Is it wrong to have doubts and fears when you take a big risk, even when you trust the person you are with? Or is that just a healthy, practical, safe way to live?
- Do you think Jesus is being a bit harsh with Peter? After all, Peter did get out of the boat and walk on the water! Or do you think Jesus is justified in his comment, because Peter is already doing the impossible?

A boat is often used as a symbol of the church. In this story it is easy to understand the symbolism of Jesus coming across the stormy waters and winds of modern times in order to help the church stay afloat.

- What do you think are the biggest problems for the church today? What is causing the worst storm?
- Are you afraid we will all sink? Do you think we will be rescued? Do you think most concerned people will jump off the boat and weather the storm of life alone or on some other type of craft? What do you think will happen?

For Children

Peter and his friends are really scared. They are on a little boat in the middle of the lake, and there is a terrible storm. It is very windy, and the boat keeps getting rocked and thrown all around. But then Jesus shows up. He comes to them, walking on the water!

- Have you ever seen anyone walk on water? Why is that so hard to do?
- Do you know how to swim in deep water?
Not only is Jesus walking on the water, but he asks Peter to come walking out on the water too!
- Do you think Peter is brave to try it? Why do you think Peter becomes afraid?
- If you saw Jesus standing on the water in the middle of a storm, and he asked you to come walk on the water with him, would you be afraid to try? Would you do it?

Closing

Some day, after we have mastered the winds, the waves, the tides and gravity, we shall harness the energies of love. Then, for the second time in the history of the world, [we] will have discovered fire. —Teilhard de Chardin

(Random Acts of Kindness)

Twentieth Sunday of the Year

The readings for this Sunday do not occur in 1999.

18 August 2002
14 August 2005

The Faith of the Gentile Woman

Scripture

- *Isaiah 56:1,6–7.* Even foreigners will be welcomed to salvation; all peoples will be accepted into the house of prayer.
- *Romans 11:13–15,29–32.* Paul is the Apostle to the Gentiles, and he intensifies that ministry to show that God is equally merciful to the Gentiles and the Jews.
- *Matthew 15:21–28.* The faith of this Gentile woman, who is turned away by the disciples, earns her not only a cure for her daughter but also a high compliment from Jesus, despite his first impression of her.

Theme

Gentiles are no longer outsiders. Isaiah proclaims that they are welcomed to the holy mountain, and Paul affirms them as his favorites, despite the jealousy of some Jews. Even though Jews are taught to despise Gentiles for their unholy ways, Jesus finally gives this Gentile woman high praise and heals her daughter.

Focusing Object
A toy dog or a picture of a dog

Reflections

For Adults

It is hard to believe these harsh words come from Jesus. He might be mimicking the attitude of the Jewish bystanders. Whatever the reason, this strong, faithful woman will not be shamed. Her love for her daughter and her faith in the miracles of this healer make her persist in her conversation with Jesus. She reminds him that even a dog eats the scraps from the table of its master. The disciples try to get rid of this pesky woman too, perhaps because she is not Jewish.

- What do you make of this story? Are you surprised by Jesus' reaction?
- Have you ever stood up to injustice—not necessarily directed at yourself but perhaps directed at another, more vulnerable person who was not being treated in the way she or he deserved? If so, what happened?
- Jesus tells this woman how great her faith is. Contrast this comment with what Jesus says to Peter in last week's Gospel passage about how small his faith is. How big or small is your faith?

For Teenagers

In Jesus' time the Jewish faith had very strict dietary laws regarding what foods could be eaten and what kinds of dishes the food could be eaten from. On the other hand, Gentiles could eat anything. Some Jews likened them to dogs, who would often be given leftover food to eat off the ground. So when Jesus and this woman speak about children and dogs, they are definitely talking about the Jews and the Gentiles.

- This Gentile woman is brave, standing up to the disciples and even to Jesus. She has a point to make, and they listen. Have you ever been that persistent in a conversation with someone who had "higher" status than you? If so, what happened?

- Does our society think of some people as "dogs"? If so, who are the dogs of our society? Who is seen as holding lower status? What is your usual response to people such as these? What would be the Christian response that Jesus calls us to? What makes that such a difficult response?
- Do you have any close friends who are Jewish? If you have friends who are Orthodox Jews, then they still obey certain dietary rules. Have you ever heard them talk of kosher foods? What kinds of things do they eat?

For Children

Jesus and his friends are Jews. Everyone else who isn't a Jew is called a Gentile. Jews don't eat certain foods that they think are impure. Jews think that Gentiles are impure because they eat these foods. So sometimes the Jews say that the Gentiles are like dogs, because dogs eat any kind of food, even if it is on the ground.
- Do you think it is nice or nasty for the Jews to say that Gentiles are like dogs?
- Do you have a dog? Do you know anyone else who does? Do the dogs you know like to eat their own dog food? Or do they prefer to eat the extra food that falls from the table?

Closing

Injustice anywhere is a threat to justice everywhere. —Martin Luther King Jr.

(The Promise of a New Day)

Twenty-First Sunday of the Year

22 August 1999
25 August 2002
21 August 2005

The Keys to the Kingdom

Scripture

- *Isaiah 22:15,19–23.* One person's authority is replaced when another person is judged more worthy.
- *Romans 11:33–36.* Paul gives up trying to understand the incredible and awesome wisdom and knowledge of God. It is too much to fathom! All he can do is sing a hymn of praise to the wonder of such a God.
- *Matthew 16:13–20.* People are confused about who Jesus is. But Peter knows he is the Messiah. Jesus compliments Peter, saying that he is the rock upon whom the church shall be built, and that he is entrusted with the keys of heaven.

Theme

The Gospel suggests that the key to knowing who Jesus is lies in using the power to forgive others. We all have that power. To experience forgiving another person is to experience the forgiving power of Jesus and to know who Jesus is and what his kingdom is like.

Focusing Object
A set of keys upon a rock

Reflections

So many others fail, but Peter answers the question correctly! He knows that Jesus is the Chosen One. The reward for his faith is great. He is the rock, entrusted with the keys. Yet Peter's faith has not been exemplary. In Matthew's Gospel, just a few verses later, Jesus says that Peter is a satan trying to get in his way. In Matthew's Gospel, two chapters earlier, Jesus asks Peter why he has such little faith. Peter is also the one who denies Jesus three times after his arrest, the night before the Crucifixion.

- Peter's faith seems to be so easily shaken. Why do you think Jesus gives the keys of heaven to him?
- What does this say about our faith and our responsibilities? Is your faith easily shaken? Which do you have more of—faith or doubts?
- Why do you think Jesus repeatedly asks his followers not to tell anyone that he is the Messiah?

For Teenagers

Keys are a symbol of trust and authority, along with responsibility.

- When have you been given keys? Do you have a key to your family's house? your family's car? your place of work? a room at school? What responsibility comes with being entrusted with a key?
- Have you ever locked your keys in a car? Have you ever locked yourself out of the house? If so, how did it happen? How did you feel? What did you do?

A rock is a symbol of solidness and strength. Rocks are hard to break, but they can break other things easily.

- Why is a rock a good symbol for faith?
- How would you describe your own faith? Is it as strong as a rock? Or is it more like a soft, weak substance, such as mashed potatoes, shaving cream, or a dried-out, crumbling leaf?

Peter isn't perfect. Remember, before Jesus is crucified, Peter denies him three times, just as Jesus predicted he would. Yet Jesus trusts him to be the leader of his disciples.

- Why would Jesus trust Peter to be the leader of his disciples?
- If being perfect is not a condition for having faith, what are the qualities that mark a strong faith?

For Children

Peter believes that Jesus is the Savior sent by God. So Jesus says that Peter's faith is as strong as a rock.

- What does it mean to have faith that is as strong as a rock? Is a rock very strong?
- What's the biggest rock you ever saw? What's the smallest rock? Can a small rock still be strong? Can a small person still be strong?

Jesus tells Peter that he has the keys to the kingdom of heaven. People who have keys are usually in charge of things and are very responsible.

- Do you think that Jesus actually hands to Peter a set of keys that he can hold in his hand and that can actually open up doors in heaven? Or do you think that Jesus is saying that Peter is responsible and will be in charge of things after Jesus leaves?
- Do you have any keys? If so, what do they open?

Closing

Feed your faith and your doubts will starve to death. —E. C. McKenzie

(Action 2000: C Cycle)

Twenty-Second Sunday of the Year

29 August 1999
1 September 2002
28 August 2005

True Discipleship

Scripture

- *Jeremiah 20:7–9.* Burdened by the hardships of following God's way, Jeremiah complains of how difficult his life is. Yet he admits that he cannot help but continue. God's love burns in him, and he must respond.
- *Romans 12:1–2.* Paul asks the disciples in Rome to take a clear look at how they live and not to let the influences of their culture stop them from doing the right thing.
- *Matthew 16:21–27.* Peter does not want Jesus to go forward into Jerusalem and suffer. Jesus rebukes him and warns the disciples about the difficulty of true discipleship.

Theme

Peer pressure is tough on any person, of any age and in any age. It is tough on Jeremiah, who is mocked and humiliated. It is tough on Paul and the early church. It is tough on Peter and Jesus. But the message is clear: To be a disciple, we must pick up our cross and carry it. We must lose our life if we wish to save it. Discipleship is not easy, but it is the only way.

Focusing Object

A simple cross

Reflections

For Adults

Peter so often seems to shoot his mouth off, not knowing what he is talking about. But he does it with great confidence. No wonder he is such a beloved saint—he probably reminds us of ourselves. He makes a lot of mistakes, but he keeps plugging away. Jesus sticks with him, and he turns out all right.

- How is Peter like a rebellious child? Does he remind you of anyone you know—anyone in your family or workplace?

The cross is a symbol of dying, but it is also a symbol of the path to rising. If we cannot accept the suffering of discipleship, then we cannot experience the glory of discipleship either.

- What are some of the hardships of discipleship that you experience in your life?
- According to Jesus, trying to save our life would mean losing it; yet losing our life for Jesus means saving it. Does this make sense to you? Why or why not?

For Teenagers

The world is full of peer pressure. It doesn't go away when you grow out of your teen years.

- How are TV commercials and ad campaigns forms of peer pressure? What do they try to persuade us to do? How successful are they?
- How are movies that contain a lot of violence or sexual activity forms of peer pressure? What do they persuade us to do? How successful are they?
- How are the church and the Gospel message forms of peer pressure? How does the faith community try to persuade us to live? How successful is that effort? Why?

Being a disciple of Jesus' is not easy, because the world is filled with all kinds of temptations and negative messages, right alongside the support and the positive messages.

- What are some negative messages in the real world that are hard to avoid? What's the secret to ignoring negative messages?
- What are some positive messages in the real world? How can you support the positive messages? What would make them even more effective?

For Children

When someone tries to get us to do something, that's called peer pressure. If someone wants us to do a good thing, then that's good peer pressure. And if someone tries to get us to do something bad, then that's called bad peer pressure. Jesus wants us to be careful about what peer pressure tells us to do.

- If someone is trying to get us to do a bad thing, it's not always easy to say no. Sometimes it seems easier just to go along with it. What can we say to a person who is trying to get us to do something wrong?

Jesus died on the cross because some people used bad peer pressure and convinced others that Jesus was a bad man. So the cross is a symbol of what can go wrong if bad peer pressure gets out of hand.

- What would you have said if you had been there in Jesus' time and someone was trying to get you to believe that Jesus was bad and should be crucified? How could you have used good peer pressure in that situation?

Closing

If you think about it, everything in life is like a banana. Nothing is straight or logical. —Thomas Baumgartel

(Success Every Day)

Twenty-Third Sunday of the Year

5 September 1999
8 September 2002
4 September 2005

Righting Wrongs

Scripture

- *Ezekiel 33:7–9.* If a person does not attempt to bring a positive influence to the wicked situations of the world, then that person is responsible for the wickedness. If a person attempts to bring a positive influence, then that person is not responsible for the wickedness, even if he or she is not successful.
- *Romans 13:8–10.* All the Commandments can be summed up with the commandment to love others, because love does not harm the loved.
- *Matthew 18:15–20.* Jesus says that in trying to right wrongs, first try to do so one-on-one. If you are not successful, try it with the support of several others. If you are still not successful, gather the help of the whole faith community. Jesus says that he is present whenever two or three are gathered in his name.

Theme

We are responsible for ourselves, our world, and one another. If we are not part of the solution, then we are part of the problem. We don't even have to be successful, as long as we faithfully and lovingly do our best and give our all. But if we don't do our best and give our all, then we are responsible for the problem and all its consequences. Whenever two or three join together in prayer, Jesus' presence is assured.

Focusing Object
Three dolls

Reflections

For Adults

These readings contain a lot of advice on how to deal with wrongs and wickedness. We are to be gentle and loving, yet to persevere in our efforts to right wrongs.

- When have you ever attempted to right a wrong in your family? with a friend? in the public? What means have you used? How successful were you?

The image of two or three gathered in prayer is a strong one. Jesus promises to be present, and he promises that the prayers will be answered.

- Do you think that any prayer you pray with one or two other people will be answered? Do you think we have that much power and control over the course of events in this world? Why or why not?

- It is often said that when a person prays about a situation, it is not the situation that is changed but the person who is praying that is changed. That is the way many prayers are answered. How do you think prayer works to change things?

For Teenagers

Ezekiel and Jesus both have good advice for dealing with people when wrong things are done.

- How easy is it to confront a friend when you think you have been wronged or treated badly? Do you tend to ignore the wrong? Do you talk about it honestly? Or do you tend to hold a grudge?

- Does the advice in today's readings relate to today's situations, or do you think we need to look at other alternatives when dealing with modern wrongs? How so?

Jesus assures us that whenever two or three pray together, Jesus is always there, and our prayers are always answered.

- Do you think that prayers are always answered? Or do you think it depends on the type of prayer and what is asked for? Or do you think that prayers are always answered, but sometimes the answer is no? How do you think prayer works?
- What kind of prayers do you most often pray? Do your prayers ask for something? Do you pray for strength and guidance? Do you ever pray with one or two others?

For Children

Jesus tells us that if someone we know is doing something wrong, we should try to talk to that person and get her or him to stop doing it and to do the right thing instead.

- Have you ever tried to get someone to stop doing a wrong thing and to do a right thing instead? If so, was it hard to do? Did it work? What happened?

Jesus also tells us that whenever two or three people pray together, he will always be there.

- Do you ever pray with another person or two? If so, when? Where? What are your prayers like?
- Do you think that Jesus is with you even when you pray by yourself? Why or why not?

Closing

It is in the shelter of each other that the people live. —An Irish proverb

(Random Acts of Kindness)

Twenty-Fourth Sunday of the Year

12 September 1999
15 September 2002
11 September 2005

Forgiveness

Scripture

- *Sirach 27:30 — 28:7.* Sinners hold onto wrath and anger, even though those feelings are hateful and destructive. It is better to forgive so that we might be forgiven.
- *Romans 14:7–9.* Paul reminds the disciples in Rome that they are not their own master, but that they answer to God.
- *Matthew 18:21–35.* Jesus says that people need to forgive others not just seven times but seventy times seven times, and he tells a story to illustrate the place that forgiveness has in the Reign of God.

Theme

Forgiveness is paramount. If we do not forgive, we become hateful and bitter, and our anger lasts and lasts. The Reign of God is like that of a ruler who forgives a servant a huge debt without even thinking, but if that servant does not show forgiveness to others, then holds the servant accountable. We always answer to God. If we want God's forgiveness, then we must forgive others as well.

Focusing Object
Seven pennies

Reflections

There can be no question about this message. If we want God to be forgiving toward us, then we must be forgiving toward others. Forgiving someone who commits a wrong seven times seems to be quite generous, especially if the Jews are thinking of the Hebrew Scriptures Book of Amos. Amos proclaims that certain crimes committed just three or four times are not going to be forgiven. Forgiving some-one seven times seems merciful.

But Jesus demands much more of us.

- Who do you find it hard to forgive? How can you get to the point where forgiveness is possible? What does forgiveness take?

Forgiveness of a crime doesn't mean that it was all right for that crime to have been committed. It means that the forgiver is no longer going to spend energy on hatred and anger related to the crime and to the person being forgiven. It actually frees up the forgiver as much as it does the forgiven, for anger and hatred are a very heavy burden that drains a person and affects the person's whole life.

- Are any crimes unforgivable? What might they be? Do you think people who commit such crimes are really aware of what they are doing, or do you think they must be deeply disturbed psycho-logically?
- What would Jesus say about unforgivable crimes and unforgivable people?

Jesus is pretty clear about forgiving people. Seventy times seven is a lot of times—four hundred and ninety times, to be exact!

- Can you imagine forgiving someone that many times, if they hurt you that many times? Why or why not?
- Can you imagine Jesus forgiving someone that many times? Why or why not?

Forgiveness of a crime doesn't mean that it was okay for that crime to have been committed. It means that the forgiver is no longer going to spend energy on hatred and anger related to the crime and to the person being forgiven. It actually frees up the forgiver as much as it does the forgiven, for anger and hatred are a very heavy burden that drains a person and affects the person's whole life.

- Because you forgive someone, does it necessarily mean that you trust that person again? If you have to forgive someone seven times for a crime, is it healthy or smart to continue to trust that person?
- Would Jesus want you to continue a close relationship with that person, or would he just ask you to give up on the anger and hatred and get on with your life?

For Children

Jesus says that when someone does something wrong, we need to forgive them, even if it happens a lot.

- When you do something wrong, do you say, "I'm sorry"? Do you usually feel forgiven after you say that?
- When someone hurts you, do they usually say, "I'm sorry"? Do you usually forgive them after that?
- What about someone who hurts you and doesn't say, "I'm sorry"? Do you usually forgive them, or do you usually stay mad at them? What would Jesus ask you to do in that situation? Is it easy or hard to do what Jesus would ask?

Closing

Who has not forgiven an enemy has not yet tasted one of the most sublime enjoyments of life.
—John Kaspar Lavater

(Vision 2000: A Cycle)

Twenty-Fifth Sunday of the Year

19 September 1999
22 September 2002
18 September 2005

The Vineyard Owner and the Workers

Scripture

- *Isaiah 55:6–9.* Isaiah says that God's ways are not what is usually expected. God will always be there when called upon.
- *Philippians 1:20–24,27.* In prison and facing possible execution, Paul compares the relative value of staying alive and working, with the value of dying and being glorified with Christ.
- *Matthew 20:1–16.* Jesus tells the parable of the vineyard owner and the workers. Everyone receives a full day's wage, even those who work only the last hour.

Theme

Paul sees nothing but good coming from his fate—whether he lives and keeps encouraging the established churches to grow, or dies and experiences the joy of being with Christ. Either way he wins. Isaiah encourages us to seek out God; no matter what evil is in our past, God will still forgive us and welcome us. No matter what, we will win. Jesus tells us that it does not matter when we join up to do the work of God's vineyard—whether we join early or late—either way we win. That's how generous God is.

Focusing Object

Grapes

For Adults

The story of the vineyard owner and the workers, which appears only in Matthew's Gospel, can be very troubling to us. A worker who comes in late in the afternoon gets the same pay that I get, even though I have been working all day. How is that fair? I deserve more! Yet I was given the very amount I was promised. Why am I so jealous when this master is so generous?

- Has this ever happened to you? Have you ever received a stipend or a raise in pay, only to find out that someone who did less work or who had less seniority than you received the same amount as well? If so, what was your reaction? What would be your reaction now?

- If we get what we are promised, why does it seem so wrong for someone who has done less to get as much compensation as we receive? Why do we become jealous if someone is overly generous to another person?

A deeper look at this parable might reveal that it isn't about corporate management, but about the Reign of God. Serious sinners who repent late in life can still be forgiven and rewarded with eternal life, just as can mild sinners who have lived a fairly good life all along. For the early church, Gentiles who became Christians late in life were not to be regarded as holding lower status than the faithful Jews who had followed the Law all along.

- How are God's ways different from human ways when it comes to justice?

- Do you think human society could survive if God's ways of justice and equity were followed?

For Teenagers

The parable of the vineyard owner and the workers doesn't always play out in the real world as cleanly as we might wish it to. It often bothers us.

- Would it bother you if you worked at a car wash or a bakery all day, and another young person who showed up an hour before closing time received the same pay as you did? Why or why not?

- Would it bother you if you worked for a week typing up a wonderful English essay, and received an A for your grade, and then you found out that someone else who scribbled their essay on scrap paper during lunch period and handed it in late also received an A? Why or why not?

- If we work hard and do well, why are we jealous if someone else does well also—especially if we think that they have not worked as hard as we have?

This parable is not exactly about an effective workplace or school policy. It's really about the way God forgives. If we have a small sin, we are forgiven. If we have a really huge sin, we are forgiven just as much.

- Does the "equal forgiveness for the unequal sin" policy seem easier to take or harder to take than the "equal pay for unequal work" or the "equal grade for unequal work" policy? Explain.

- Does this mean that we can go out and commit tremendous sins and do reckless things and hurt people we care about because, in the end, we will be forgiven just the same anyway? What is wrong with this plan? What would Jesus say about this?

For Children

Jesus tells us a story about a landowner who hires many workers to cut down the grapes from the vines when they become ripe. The workers who work the entire day are paid well. But the workers who work only a few hours are paid the same amount.

- If you had picked grapes all day in a field, and you received fifty dollars, would you be happy with that pay? Why or why not?

- What if you found out that the children who came in after lunch and only picked grapes for two hours also received fifty dollars? Would you be mad about it? Or would you think that was okay too?
- Let's change the situation. Suppose you were busy in the morning, and you came to the vineyard as soon as you could. You picked grapes for two hours, and by then all the grapes had been picked, and you received fifty dollars for just two hours of work. Would you be happy with that pay? Why or why not?
- What would you say if someone who had been working there all day got angry with you because the boss gave you so much money? Would you still want to keep the money? Why or why not?

Closing

I wept because I had no shoes, until I saw someone who had no feet. —An ancient Persian saying
(Vision 2000: A Cycle)

Twenty-Sixth Sunday of the Year

26 September 1999
29 September 2002
25 September 2005

Two Children and Their Opposite Responses

Scripture

- *Ezekiel 18:25–28.* This teaching clarifies that when virtuous people turn to sin, they will suffer, and when wicked people turn to virtue, they will not suffer.
- *Philippians 2:1–11.* An ancient hymn that we hear every year on Palm Sunday says that every knee must bend and every tongue must proclaim that Jesus Christ is Lord.
- *Matthew 21:28–32.* This parable, which only appears in Matthew's Gospel, speaks of two children and how differently they respond to their parent's request.

Theme

Paul reminds us that Jesus humbled himself and followed the way of God. We are to do the same. If we say we are believers, then we must not stray and do wicked things. If we are wicked, then we must change our ways and become believers. Isaiah and Jesus both point out that being called virtuous believers is not enough. We will be judged on what we actually do.

Focusing Object
Two dolls or figurines, placed back-to-back

Reflections

Can you imagine an outside preacher coming to your parish and telling your pastor, "I know tax collectors and prostitutes who will get to heaven in front of you!" Wouldn't that be a scandal?

- What would be the conditions for a prostitute or other "sinner" to get to heaven before a pastor?
- Jesus asks us to see ourselves in the parable two children and their different responses to a parent. If it doesn't shake us up, then we probably aren't listening. What would our response be if we took the message of this reading seriously?

Appearing as if you are a good Christian—obedient to God and faithful to the Gospels—does not guarantee a place in heaven. Appearances mean nothing. Some pretty decent people may look evil to us, and some people may look holy to us but be evil to the core.

- Have there been situations in which you felt your appearance and your true self were different? What is it like to be in that space? What would Jesus say about that discrepancy?
- If you have children, which of these two Gospel children do your children most often imitate? Do they more often say the "yes" and do the "no"? Or do they more often say the "no" and do the "yes"?
- Are you doubly blessed with a "say yes–do yes" child?
- When you were a child, which were you more likely to be?

These are fierce words that Jesus gives us: that tax collectors and prostitutes are entering heaven in greater numbers than are priests and appointed elders! But Jesus is talking about priests and elders who are like the child who outwardly says, "Yes!" to God, yet doesn't really do God's work. The tax collectors and prostitutes are like the child who outwardly says, "No!" to God, yet does the best he or she can in any situation.

- At home, which child are you more like? Are you more likely to say you'll do something, and then not do it? Or are you more likely to talk back to your parents, but later do what they ask anyway? Or do you do both? Explain your answer and give some examples.
- Do you respond at school in the same way as you do at home, or differently?
- How are you at work? Are you more likely to say yes and not do the task, or are you more likely to say no but then do the work anyway?
- What might Jesus be saying to you with this parable?

For Children

Jesus tells us a story about two children. Probably you know what it's like to be each of these children.

- When have you gotten mad at your mother or father and said you wouldn't do something, but later went ahead and did it anyway because you knew it was the right thing to do?
- When have you told your mother or father you would do something, but later either forgot or changed your mind, and just didn't do it?

Jesus might say that the best thing would be for you to tell your mother or father, "Yes, I will do what you say," and then actually do it.

- When have you done that?

Closing

Children have never been good at listening to their elders, but they have never failed to imitate them. —James Baldwin

(Mission 2000: B Cycle)

Twenty-Seventh Sunday of the Year

3 October 1999
6 October 2002
2 October 2005

Jesus, the Cornerstone

Scripture

- *Isaiah 5:1–7.* Isaiah sings a song about God, his "friend" who lovingly cares for a vineyard, yet the fruit it bears is of very low quality.
- *Philippians 4:6–9.* Paul recommends that we let go of anxiety and accept God's own peace.
- *Matthew 21:33–43.* Jesus tells a parable about the tenant farmers who kill the son of the vineyard owner. Often the cornerstone (or keystone) is rejected by the very builders of the structure.

Theme

The vineyard story in Isaiah compliments the vineyard story in Matthew. In the first story, God cares for a vineyard, and the fruit (the people) is not sweet but bitter. In the Gospel, God cares for a vineyard, but at harvest time the farmers kill the vineyard owner's son (Jesus). Jesus reminds the listeners that this story echoes Psalm 188, which proclaims the value of the rejected cornerstone. Paul urges us to live according to what we have learned and accepted, in order to be less anxious and more at peace with God.

Focusing Object

A brick or a child's building block

Reflections

Although Jesus is mixing his metaphors—vineyard, farmers, and owner's son; structure, builders, and cornerstones—the point is clear: Jesus, rejected because of his faithfulness, is to be the most prized and valued of all.

- Who is rejected most often today? Who are some of the people on the fringes of society, those ostracized by the public?
- What is your role? Are you one of the rejecters, or are you one of the supporters?

Jesus tells the chief priests and elders that the Reign of God will be taken away from them and given to a people that will yield a rich harvest.

- How are you similar to the chief priests and elders?
- How are you similar to the rejected cornerstone?
- How are you similar to the people reaping the rich harvest?
- How are you similar to the rich harvest itself?

All of us are sinners. We are all like the tenant farmers and the builders from time to time.

- Where is the hope for the world if all of us are sinners?

This parable couldn't be more obvious. The vineyard owner's son is killed by the tenants, so then the vineyard owner will lease the vineyard to different people who will care for the grapes in an honest and respectable way, in memory of his son who died. Jesus switches symbols from grapes to bricks, and then emphasizes how the cornerstone is the very stone that was initially rejected by the builders of the structure. Jesus challenges us to look deeply into this symbolism.

- Who are the rejected bricks and stones at your school? Are there any outcast students who are mocked by others? Why are certain people judged to be more popular or less popular than others?

- What would Jesus say about the value of less-popular individuals?
- How would your reaction to them be different if you took this Gospel message seriously? Are you going to change your reaction to them? Why or why not?
- Who are the newer people that lease the land and help to harvest the grapes? Are you in this category?
- Who are the tenant farmers? Who are the builders who dislike the cornerstone? Are you in this category?

For Children

Jesus says that the most special brick in the whole building is the one that some people don't like at first. It's like saying that sometimes the nicest person is the person that nobody likes at first.
- Did you ever go someplace and feel as if nobody liked you? What happened there?
- Jesus says that even when other people don't treat you well, you are still special to Jesus. Does that help you feel any better about those times?
- At times Jesus wasn't treated very well. A lot of people disliked Jesus, even though he was the most special person in the world. Even though he is God! What kinds of nasty things did people do to Jesus?

Closing

The Church is a society of sinners. It is the only society in the world in which membership is based upon a single qualification, that the candidate be unworthy of membership. —Charles Clayton Morrison

(Vision 2000: A Cycle)

Twenty-Eighth Sunday of the Year

10 October 1999
13 October 2002
9 October 2005

All Come to the Wedding Feast

Scripture

- *Isaiah 25:6–10.* The prophet describes a marvelous feast on a mountain with God providing rich food and drink for all.
- *Philippians 4:12–14,19–20.* Paul admits that he has known abundant food as well as deep hunger. In both circumstances he has turned to God for his strength.
- *Matthew 22:1–14.* Jesus tells of the king whose invited guests have excuses and choose not to come to his son's wedding feast, so he has his servants go out and invite anyone they come upon.

Theme

Paul has known both feasting and fasting in his life, and in both situations Paul remembers God. Isaiah reminds us that our God calls us to feast. And Jesus reminds us that if we choose to decline our invitation to the Reign of God, then surely someone else will take our place.

Focusing Object
A bride-and-groom topper for a wedding cake, or any other wedding symbol

Reflections

In this parable the king is very generous with his invitations. One wonders why so many people decline their invitation to join the feast. One also wonders at the surprise of those along the road who are asked to come into the king's company.

- The invitation to the Reign of God is always open. Why do so many decline that invitation? Have you ever gone through a period when you declined God's invitation? If so, what were the circumstances?
- We don't deserve the invitation, so it often comes as a surprise. When have you been surprised and delighted by God's goodness in your life?

Some people accept the invitation in words, but they do not live the life of a heavenly guest. Their behavior is unacceptable, and they can be welcomed back in only after their life reflects a sincere acceptance of that invitation. It is not so much that they have been excluded from the party but that they have chosen to exclude themselves.

- Have you ever realized that you weren't sincerely answering yes to Jesus' invitation to follow him and become a disciple? If so, what were the circumstances? How did it all turn out?

What a story! It's not your typical wedding. The king is God. The first people invited are those who reject God's way of living. The second people are those who don't expect the invitation but are delighted when it comes, and they accept it wholeheartedly. And the person not properly dressed represents those who may say that they have accepted God's invitation, but whose life choices show that they have not yet really said yes to God.

- When have you been among the first group— those who don't care about church, who don't want to be involved with anything "churchy," and who don't think faith is relevant today? What do you think Jesus would say to you about this attitude?

- When have you been among the second group—those who see that faith is important, who try to live their faith by doing works of service, and who aren't embarrassed by their relationship with God? What do you think Jesus would say to you about this attitude?
- When have you been among the third group—those who say that faith is important and yet don't really practice their faith. What do you think Jesus would say to you about this attitude?

For Children

Jesus says that saying yes to God and doing the things that God wants us to do is like saying yes to a king who invites us to a big wedding feast.

- Have you ever been to a wedding party? If so, what was it like? Who got married?
- If you have never been to a wedding, have you ever seen a movie or a TV show about a wedding? What happens at a wedding?

People who are invited to a wedding can say, "No, I cannot come." They don't have to go if they don't want to. In the same way, when God invites us to do good things and to be the best person we can be, we have a choice. We can tell God, "Yes, I will try to do good things." Or we can tell God, "No, I don't want to do what you want me to do."

- What have you done that you know God would be happy about?
- What is something that you know God wouldn't want you to do?

Closing

He drew a circle that shut me out—
Heretic, rebel, a thing to flout.
But love and I had the wit to win.
We drew a circle that took him in.
                                    —Edwin Markham
                              (Vision 2000: A Cycle)

Twenty-Ninth Sunday of the Year

17 October 1999
20 October 2002
16 October 2005

Give Caesar's to Caesar; Give God's to God

Scripture

- *Isaiah 45:1,4–6.* Cyrus is not our Messiah, but he is called God's anointed because he is so accommodating. After conquering Babylonia, he allows the Jews exiled there to return to their homes and rebuild their lives and their temple. Isaiah sees this as part of God's plan.
- *1 Thessalonians 1:1–5.* Paul sees that the leadership of the church of Thessalonica is guided by the Holy Spirit, and he affirms the leaders as he begins this letter to them.
- *Matthew 22:15–21.* The Pharisees and the Herodians try to trap Jesus by asking him to choose between the authority of Caesar and the authority of God. Jesus refuses to choose and be trapped.

Theme

Paul and Isaiah both express faith in the Holy Spirit to carry out God's plan. Isaiah and Matthew show us that God's plan can exist side by side with a civil or governmental plan. We are wise to be mindful of the balance.

Focusing Object
A coin

Reflections

For Adults

The question of taxes is tricky indeed. The role of Caesar demands homage, and Caesar claims to have divine authority. So by asking about the taxes in this reading from Matthew, the Pharisees are hoping for Jesus to trip up and say that the taxes are fair—meaning that Caesar's divine authority is authentic. Saying that would be a sin against belief in the sovereign one true God, and so the Pharisees would be able to criticize Jesus. But the Herodians are also hoping for Jesus to trip up and say that the taxes are not fair—meaning that Caesar's authority is not authentic. Saying that would be a crime of treason against the country, and then the Herodians would be able to criticize Jesus.

- Have you ever been stuck in the middle when asked a controversial question? Have you ever had to struggle to find an answer that would not offend either side in an issue? If so, when? What did you do?

Jesus' answer demonstrates that the religious and the political need not exist as enemies. The heavenly and the earthly need not be in opposition. The two can have a peaceful and complementary cohabitation.

- Do you ever feel a tension between your political views and your religious views? If so, how do you handle that struggle?
- Do you see a separation in your life between what is of this world and what is of God? Or do you see the two as merged peacefully?

For Teenagers

The Pharisees and the Herodians try to trip Jesus up, but he won't fall for their setup. They ask him to choose between the worldly and the holy, between the political and the religious. Jesus simply says that we need to give to each what is due to each.

- Do you ever experience a conflict between what your faith says and what your country says? If something is legal, is it always moral? And if something is moral, is it always legal? What is an example of such a conflict?
- Do you ever experience a conflict between what your civil community says and what your faith community says? If something is an acceptable practice in your school or in your circle of friends, does that mean it's always right to do? And is the right thing always acceptable in your social situation? What is an example of such a conflict? Some people try to live entirely in one arena, and they are totally against the other.
- Do you know anyone who completely rejects all religion and talk of God and only clings to the physical, modern world? What is that attitude like?
- Do you know anyone who completely rejects all earthly things and clings only to the religious and spiritual? What is that attitude like?
- Do you know anyone who lives a good balance of both the spiritual and the earthly? What is that attitude like?

For Children

Some people try to trick Jesus to get him to say that what his country says is more important than what his church says, or to say that what his faith says is more important than what his country says. But he won't be tricked. Jesus knows that both what his country says and what his church says are important.

- What is the name of the country where you live? What are some good things that happen in your country?
- What is the name of the church where you worship? What are some good things that happen in your church?

Closing

You can be so heavenly bound [that] you are no earthly good. —Dr. Oscar Lane

(Acts of Faith)

Thirtieth Sunday of the Year

24 October 1999
27 October 2002
23 October 2005

The Great Commandments

Scripture

- *Exodus 22:20–26.* The Israelites are told to be the most compassionate to the most vulnerable—foreigners, widows, orphans, and poor people.
- *1 Thessalonians 1:5–10.* The Thessalonians are praised for their faith and the practice of their faith. They imitated Paul and his followers, and now others are imitating them.
- *Matthew 22:34–40.* A lawyer tries to trip Jesus up by asking him to choose the one greatest commandment. Jesus offers two—love of God and love of neighbor.

Theme

In the Gospel, Jesus tells us that loving God is number one, but number two is loving our neighbor, and number two is very much like number one. In case we're not sure who our neighbors are, their identity is spelled out clearly for us in the first reading—anyone who needs help, anyone who does not have the power to take care of their own needs. And in case we're not sure if this works or not, the success of the Thessalonians to imitate Christ, Paul, and the other early Christians is clearly documented in the second reading. When we imitate Christ, others will imitate us. The way of Jesus works, and it is as simple as the word *love.*

Focusing Object

A heart

Reflections

For Adults

We have the Ten Commandments. The Hebrew Scripture Books of Exodus and Leviticus are filled with more laws on top of those, and the Books of Numbers and Deuteronomy have sections of laws as well. With all this effort to expand the original basic ten, Jesus is asked to limit his choice to just one. He chooses love.

- If you had to summarize all the laws of the country, all the rules of your workplace, or all the rules of your family into one basic rule, what would it be? How would your answer differ from Jesus' answer?

In the last several Gospel stories heard at Mass, Jesus has been challenging the learned. The priests and the elders, the Pharisees and the Sadducees are all feeling uncomfortable with this man who speaks with authority, who cannot be tripped up, and who has an answer for everything. In today's Gospel, Jesus speaks gently, as if he does not notice that the questioner is trying to set him up.

- Have you ever felt set up? Has anyone ever tried to trap you or make you look bad? If so, what was your reaction? If not, what might your reaction be?
- How can we learn to react the way Jesus reacts—with that same peace and confidence—even when we feel under pressure? What does love have to do with that peace and confidence?

For Teenagers

At the same time that young people want more freedom, more rules apply. More freedom just means fewer outside rules. That's because more freedom means more responsibility, and more responsibility means more inside rules—rules that we make for ourselves. For example, the Ten Commandments are outside rules—they tell us exactly what to do. Jesus' two commandments of love are inside rules—they tell us to make rules for ourselves that are motivated by love. Actually, if we make rules for ourselves that are motivated by love, our actions will follow the Ten Commandments, even if we have never heard of the Ten Commandments.

- What are some of your school rules and home rules? Are they outside rules or inside rules? If they are outside rules, summarize them with one inside rule. If any of them are inside rules, then give an outside example of how you might follow them.
- Would a society work if its only laws were inside rules? Why or why not? How would that affect this country? How would it affect your state, county, or city?

Saint Augustine is famous for saying, "Love, and then do what you will."

- How is this quote similar to what Jesus told the lawyer?
- What does love of self look like? What does love of God look like? How are those types of love related to love of neighbor?
- Do you think that when Jesus said, "Love your neighbor," he meant just the people on your street, or all people—including strangers, people in faraway countries, and even people at school that you don't get along with? How does that sit with you?

For Children

Jesus told us to love God, to love ourselves, and to love our neighbors.

- Do you love God? Do you ever talk to God?
- Do you love yourself? If so, how do you take care of yourself to show that love?
- Do you love other people? If so, whom do you love? How do you show them that you love them?

Closing

Go behind the apparent circumstances of the situation and locate the love in yourself and in all others involved in the situation. —Mother Teresa
(Acts of Faith)

Thirty-First Sunday of the Year

31 October 1999
3 November 2002
30 October 2005

Avoiding Hypocrisy

Scripture

- *Malachi 1:14—2:2,8–10.* The prophet Malachi explains that God is unhappy with the religious leaders who are not teaching faith by their example.
- *1 Thessalonians 2:7–9,13.* Paul reminds the young church of Thessalonica of his example to them of gentle care and of preaching God's Good News.
- *Matthew 23:1–12.* Jesus tells his followers to listen to the things the scribes and the Pharisees say, but not to follow the example of these religious leaders.

Theme

God has high standards for the leaders of the faith. Malachi speaks of God's anger when the scribes and the Pharisees do not give a good example for the people to follow. And Jesus criticizes the huge tassels, the places of honor at banquets, and the special titles of those trying to exalt themselves. They talk the talk, but they don't walk the walk. Paul compares doing God's work to the gentle care a mother gives her babies when fondling them and nursing them. The only great ones are the ones who serve others. The only ones who will be exalted are those who humble themselves.

Focusing Object

A medal, a ribbon, or some other prize of recognition and honor

Reflections

For Adults

In the real world, we learn that the squeaky wheel gets the oil. We learn to toot our own horn. We learn that we have to impress people with our own praises if we want to get ahead. If we try to be humble, someone else will take credit for our ideas and our work.

- Is Jesus' advice about being humble outdated for today's world? Why or why not?

We have often heard the advice, "Do as I say, not as I do." But we know that people usually judge us by what we do, not by what we say. We also know that our children imitate what they see. Jesus speaks very harshly about leaders who have bold words and weak deeds.

- In what area do you find that you talk the talk better than you walk the walk? How can you improve upon that?

For Teenagers

Jesus hates hypocrisy. It's the one sin he really nails us on. Pretending to be a saint while doing sinful deeds is what he hates the most.

- When do you pretend to be righteous and good with your words, while your actions show you to be less than that? What area can you work on?
- What does humility have to do with saintliness or sinfulness?

Jesus criticizes some religious leaders for preaching the word of God but not living it. He goes so far as to tell us to do what they say, but not to do what they do. But not all religious leaders are bad. Some of them are humble people trying to do the work that Jesus taught us to do.

- Who are the religious leaders you respect because of not only what they say but what they do?

- Who are the teachers, coaches, employers, or community leaders you know whom you respect because of what they do as well as because of what they say?

For Children

Jesus wants us to be humble. That means that he doesn't want us bragging about how great we are, he doesn't want us to boss other people around, and he doesn't want us to act as if we are better than other people. Instead of all that, he just wants us to do the right thing and to be good to people.

- Do you ever brag? Do you try to boss other people around? Do you ever act as if you are better than another person? Why do you think you do that? How does it feel to do it? How does it make other people feel? Why is it something Jesus doesn't like?
- If you always try to do the right thing and try to be good to people, what do you think people will say about you? How do you think they will feel when they are with you? Would the world be better if everyone did that? Why or why not?

Closing

The first element of greatness is fundamental humbleness. —Margot Asquith

(The Promise of a New Day)

Thirty-Second Sunday of the Year

7 November 1999
10 November 2002
6 November 2005

The Sensible and Foolish Bridesmaids

Scripture

- *Wisdom 6:12–16.* God, the source of all wisdom, is praised. God with Wisdom is always present, perceived by those who love Wisdom.
- *1 Thessalonians 4:13–18.* The author of this letter tells the Thessalonians that believing Jesus died and then rose from the dead means believing that they will also rise to life after they die. Those who sleep in death will rise again. And those who are still awake will join them when Jesus comes the second time.
- *Matthew 25:1–13.* The foolish bridesmaids do not bring extra oil with them. The sensible bridesmaids think ahead and are prepared when the coming of the groom is delayed.

Theme

Wisdom is what separates the foolish from the sensible. The foolish will not be successful. They do not look ahead and plan, so they are not ready when their opportunity comes. The sensible are wise. They look ahead, they are ready, and their opportunities are not wasted. Whether they are waiting for Jesus' Second Coming or they are waiting for a delayed groom to show up, they are prepared. Where does this wisdom come from?

It comes from God. When we look to Wisdom, she will not let us down.

Focusing Object
An oil lamp

Reflections

For Adults

God is the source of all wisdom. Wisdom is one of the major gifts of the Holy Spirit. Wisdom is what leads to success.
- In what areas of your life have you been foolish? What unfortunate consequences have you had to live with because of that foolishness?
- In what areas of your life have you been wise? What benefits of that wisdom have you enjoyed?
- How might Jesus describe success?

Being prepared for the bridegroom is like being prepared for the Messiah to come. It was surprising to the Jews that many of the Gentiles were ready, yet many of the Jews were not. Being prepared for the bridegroom is like being prepared for Jesus' Second Coming.
- How would a sensible person prepare for the Second Coming of Jesus, even though she or he may not know the day or the hour? What might a foolish person do?
- Along the continuum from wise to foolish, where do you think you fall in regard to your preparation for Jesus' Second Coming?

For Teenagers

God is the source of all wisdom. Wisdom is a gift of the Holy Spirit. Wisdom is what leads to success.
- Think of a time in your life when you weren't very wise, and you found yourself in a "no oil for the oil lamp" situation. What happened? How did you deal with the consequences?
- Think of a time when you were wise—a time when you did think ahead and were prepared—and your preparation paid off because something unexpected popped up. What happened? How did you benefit?

- Do you think that most of the young people you know tend to be on the wise side or on the foolish side? Why? Give some examples of how that affects your school, your church, your city or town, and the world.
- How would Jesus describe success?

For Children

Jesus tells the story of the bridesmaids who are waiting for the groom to come. Some of them are foolish, and they run out of oil. But the ones who remember to bring extra oil are ready when the groom comes.

- How would you feel if you were a bridesmaid and you forgot to bring extra oil for your oil lamp? What would you say when you ran out of oil? What would you try to do?
- How would you feel if you were one of the bridesmaids who remembered to bring extra oil? What would you say to the ones who were foolish and forgot to bring extra oil?
- Sometimes when we travel, we have to take things with us that we will need during our trip. What kinds of things do you have to remember to take with you? What can happen if you forget to take them?

Closing

There are four rungs on the ladder of success: Plan Purposefully, Prepare Prayerfully, Proceed Positively, Pursue Persistently. —From African-American folklore

(Acts of Faith)

Thirty-Third Sunday of the Year

14 November 1999
17 November 2002
13 November 2005

Using Our Talents

Scripture

- *Proverbs 31:10–13,19–20,30–31.* The characteristics of a hardworking woman (not her physical beauty and charm) are praised.
- *1 Thessalonians 5:1–6.* The author warns the Thessalonians to be alert and ready, for they never know when God will call them.
- *Matthew 25:14–30.* Jesus compares the actions of three servants whose master entrusted each of them with an amount of money according to their ability.

Theme

Although the Book of Proverbs was written in a patriarchal society that viewed a wife as a possession, the first reading for today still praises skill and labor above charm and beauty. This praise was countercultural at the time. In the second reading, the author warns the people not to be lazy, but to be alert and ready for the "day of the Lord" (end of the world), for they were certain that Jesus was returning to earth in their own lifetime. In the Gospel, Jesus praises the servants who take risks and work hard, not the servant who buries what he is given out of fear.

Focusing Object

Eight pennies, divided into a pile of five, a set of two, and one

Reflections

For Adults

In the parable of the master entrusting money to three servants, Jesus challenges us to do the best we can with what we are given, and not to be afraid of taking risks. If we bury our talents, we do not do much good for ourselves or for anyone else.

- When have you taken a risk, worked hard, and done very well?
- Have you ever taken a risk that didn't work out very well? Has that made you more afraid of taking risks?
- When have you been afraid to take a risk?

Besides being a message about our talents and courage, this parable may also be a message about our faith practice and our traditions.

- Regarding our faith, when are we like the third servant, who plays it safe and buries the treasure without telling anyone about it or trying to enhance it?
- Regarding our faith, when are we like the first two servants, who take a risk and try to develop the treasure, to improve upon the treasure, and to help the treasure mature?
- How would lives change if this faith message were taken more seriously?

For Teenagers

In the parable that Jesus tells in today's Gospel, the master praises the efforts of the first two servants, who used the talents they were given and improved upon them. The master criticizes the action of the third servant, who hid the talent, did nothing, and was paralyzed with fear.

- When have you been like the first and second servants, using your talents in a way that benefits yourself and others?

- When have you been like the third servant, not using your talents and not bringing benefit to yourself or others?

The last few lines of this Gospel passage might seem to contradict Jesus' usual message about the last being first. This passage appears to be saying that the first will be even further ahead, and the last will be left behind.

- Is this contradiction troubling to you? Why or why not? How do you see it?
- When Jesus speaks of the first becoming last and the last becoming first, he is usually speaking of humility and boastfulness. Those who pump themselves up are usually just full of hot air. Why would Jesus say that the humble ones are really the great ones?
- When Jesus speaks of the rich ones getting more, and the poor ones losing what they have, he is speaking in terms of laziness and activity. Those who act lazy usually become more lazy, and they lose any initiative they once had. What kind of activity is Jesus encouraging us to do?

For Children

- Retell the Gospel story for today, using fifteen pennies. First divide the eight pennies into sets of five, two, and one; then add five pennies to the set of five, add two pennies to the set of two, and remove the one penny.

Jesus wants us to use our talents. He wants us to find out what we are good at and what we can do well. Then he wants us to do those things to help other people and to make the world better.

- Some people like to draw. Some like to dance. Some like to run or swim or ride their bicycle or play ball. Some like to read books. Some like to take care of animals. Some like to sing. What do you like to do?
- What might be your favorite way to help people and to make the world better? What would Jesus say about this?

Closing

Even if you're on the right track, you'll get run over if you just sit there. —Will Rogers

(Success Every Day)

Thirty-Fourth Sunday of the Year (Christ the King)

21 November 1999
24 November 2002
20 November 2005

The
Judgment

Scripture

- *Ezekiel 34:11–12,15–17.* God promises to take care of the flock. God also promises to judge between the sheep and the rams and the goats.
- *1 Corinthians 15:20–26,28.* At the end of the world, the Reign of God will be obvious, and Jesus will rise above all enemies.
- *Matthew 25:31–46.* At the end of time, Jesus will see the sheep and goats divided. The division will be based on how each person served those in need.

Theme

The feast of Christ the King is the last Sunday of Ordinary Time. Next Sunday begins Advent, and we begin the new year of the B cycle of readings. So on this last Sunday, we focus on last things—on the end of the world, on the Last Judgment, and on Jesus, who will see the division of the sheep and the goats. Ezekiel and Paul both warn us about it, and Jesus' warning is similar. The time will come when each of us must be held accountable for what we have and have not done.

Focusing Object

A toy sheep and toy goat, or pictures of a sheep and a goat

Reflections

For Adults

Predictions for the end of the world can be both frightening and entertaining.

- Do you remember the first time you heard of some prophet or religious group predicting the end of the world? Were you concerned? How did you feel about it? How does that compare with the way you react to such predictions now?
- How would you respond to a child or young person who is concerned about such predictions?
- What concerns you more—the end of the world or your own death? Do you consider yourself prepared for either one of them—or both of them? Why or why not?

Some people question the existence of hell, and they doubt that an all-loving and all-merciful God would send anyone there.

- Do you believe in a hell of eternal punishment for those who have sinned seriously while on earth? Why or why not?
- If every person, at death, comes face-to-face with Jesus and has to answer the questions of justice (When did you feed me, give me drink, welcome me, clothe me, or visit me?), do you think their self-judgment will be any different from Jesus' judgment of them? If so, how?
- What might actually condemn a person to suffer eternal punishment—an angry God seeking revenge? or an embarrassed and shamed person seeking to escape and hide?

For Teenagers

Jesus never really declared himself to be king of anything on earth. But we declare him to be our king.

- How is Jesus like an earthly king?
- How is he different from an earthly king?

Every so often you read in the paper or see on television that some famous person or religious group is predicting the end of the world.

- How do you feel when you hear such predictions? Are you concerned? Are you fascinated? Are you troubled? How so?
- What would you be more afraid of—the sudden end of the world or your sudden death? How do both of these events affect you when you consider their actual possibility?

For Children

The Gospel story for today is a hard story for us to hear. Jesus tells us that he will separate people into two groups in the way a shepherd separates the sheep from the goats. The two groups of people will be those who mostly do good things and those who mostly do bad things. The people who mostly do good things and live in the way that Jesus wants them to will come into heaven and live with him forever.

- What kinds of good things do you do that Jesus would be happy about? Who are the people that you help?
- If everybody in the whole world does good things, then everybody gets to go to heaven. Do you think that could happen? Why or why not?

Closing

Know thy ideal and live for that. For each soul must give an account for its own self.
—Paramhansa Yogananda

(Acts of Faith)

Index by Theme

Theme	Scripture	Pages

Jesus teaches:

Theme	Scripture	Pages
A pearl of great price	Matthew 13:44–52	70–72
Reconcile before laying your gift at the altar	Matthew 5:17–37	34–36
A stone rejected by the builders	Matthew 21:33–43	102–104
Two or three gather in my name	Matthew 18:15–20	89–91
We are more important than sparrows	Matthew 10:26–33	54–56
A wedding banquet	Matthew 22:1–14	105–107
Weeds and wheat	Matthew 13:24–43	67–69
Which child obeyed the parent?	Matthew 21:28–32	99–101
Workers of the vineyard	Matthew 20:1–16	95–98
Worry not; God will provide	Matthew 6:24–34	40–43

Index by Focusing Object

Acknowledgments *(continued)*

The excerpts on pages 17, 50, 59, 72, 94, 98, 104, and 107 are from *Vision 2000: Praying Scripture in a Contemporary Way: A Cycle,* by Mark Link, SJ (Allen, TX: Tabor Publishing, 1992), pages 161, 50, 15, 61, 210, 201, 162, and 149, respectively. Copyright © 1992 by Mark Link.

The excerpts on pages 21, 43, 76, and 85 are from *Action 2000: Praying Scripture in a Contemporary Way: C Cycle,* by Mark Link, SJ (Allen, TX: Tabor Publishing, 1992), pages 324, 197, 60, and 97, respectively. Copyright © 1992 by Mark Link.

The excerpts on pages 24, 53, 62, 110, 113, 119, and 126 are from *Acts of Faith: Meditations for People of Color,* by Iyanla Vanzant (New York: Simon and Schuster, Fireside Book, 1993), n.pp. Copyright © 1993 by Iyanla Vanzant.

The excerpts on pages 27, 79, and 91 are from *Random Acts of Kindness,* by the editors of Conari Press (Berkeley, CA: Conari Press, 1993), pages 18, 53, and 82, respectively. Copyright © 1993 by Conari Press.

The quote by Abraham Lincoln on page 30 is taken from a greeting card message.

The excerpts on pages 33, 46, and 69 are from *Familiar Quotations,* 14th ed., by John Bartlett, edited by Emily Morison Beck (Boston: Little, Brown and Company, 1968), pages 930, 641, and 789, respectively. Copyright © 1968 by Little, Brown and Company.

The excerpts on pages 36, 56, 82, and 116 are from *The Promise of a New Day,* by Karen Casey and Martha Vanceburg (New York: HarperCollins Publishers, Hazelden Book, 1983), n.pp. Copyright © 1983 by the Hazelden Foundation.

The excerpts on pages 39, 88, and 123 are from *Success Every Day,* by Weight Watchers (New York: Macmillan General Reference, 1996), n.pp. Copyright © 1996 by Weight Watchers International.

The excerpt on page 66 is taken from *Days of Healing, Days of Joy: Daily Meditations for Adult Children,* by Ernie Larsen and Carol Larsen Hegarty (New York: Harper and Row, Publishers, 1987), n.p. Copyright © 1987 by the Hazelden Foundation.